ASPECTS
OF ANTIQUITY

Discoveries and Controversies

by

M. I. Finley

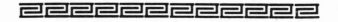

D1497244

New York   The Viking Press

To
J. H. PLUMB

Acknowledgements

The essays in this volume have, with the exception of 'Diogenes the Cynic', all been published previously, in somewhat different form. 'Plato and Practical Politics', 'The Emperor Diocletian', and 'Manpower and the Fall of Rome' appeared in *The Listener*, London; 'Desperately Foreign' and 'Silver Tongue' in *The New Statesman*, London; '*Etruscheria*' and 'Christian Beginnings' in *The New York Review of Books*, New York; and the rest in *Horizon*, New York. Thanks are due to the editors and to the publishers of the respective publications, for permission to reprint these essays, which in some cases have been retitled.

The essays have all been revised and expanded since their original publication, some substantially. For help in preparing this volume I have to thank my pupil, Richard Gordon of Jesus College, Cambridge.

M. I. F.

Cambridge
1967

CONTENTS

MAPS

PLATES

ASPECTS OF ANTIQUITY

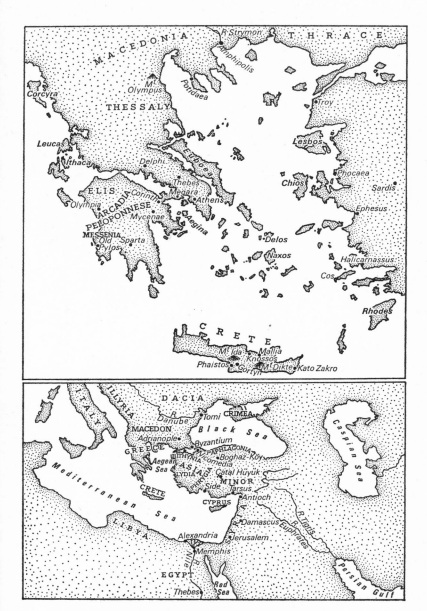

GREECE AND WESTERN ASIA

DESPERATELY FOREIGN

IN the course of a very long passage midway through *Oedipus the King* the chorus of Theban elders says:

I will go no more to Apollo's inviolate shrine. . . . The old prophecies about Laius are losing their power; already men are dismissing them from mind, and Apollo is nowhere glorified with honours. *Religion is dying.*

The "old prophecies" refer to the oracle which promised that Laius, king of Thebes, would be murdered by his son, who would then marry Laius's widow, his own mother. In fact, all this had long since come to pass, though neither the old men nor Oedipus nor Jocasta knew it yet. "Religion is dying" not because of revulsion against a god who decreed such a fate for a child still unborn, but on the contrary because what a god had prophesied seemed not to be fulfilled; worse, seemed to have been successfully thwarted by human artifice. "When Sophocles makes his Chorus of Theban elders" say this, writes Mr John Jones in *On Aristotle and Greek Tragedy,** "we should allow them to mean what they say."

It is no easy matter to let either the Greek tragedians or Aristotle on tragedy mean what they say. Too many generations, even centuries, of interpretation stand in the way despite some notable protests past and present, and it has required all of Mr Jones's very considerable intellectual powers, rigorously disciplined reading of texts, and brilliant expository gifts to bring us back to something plausibly authentic. The starting-point is Aristotle's *Poetics*; and of the *Poetics*, one of its simplest sentences: "Tragedy is an imitation not of human beings but of action and life." Allow Aristotle

* (London: Chatto & Windus; New York: Oxford University Press, 1962).

to mean what he says and the first victim is the tragic hero, to be largely discarded together with such corollaries as the debate over who *is* the hero in many of the Greek plays.

Aristotle is assaulting the now settled habit in which we see action issuing from a solitary focus of consciousness— secret, inward, interesting. . . . To our sense of characteristic conduct Aristotle opposes that of characterful action; the essence of conduct being that it is mine or yours; of action, that it is out there—an object for men to contemplate.

This is perhaps not easy. But Mr Jones does not leave us to wrestle with abstract propositions. He makes a concrete demonstration (of this and many other ideas, both Aristotelian and non-Aristotelian) by taking us through play after play. In none is the point about action more obvious than in *Oedipus the King*. The beginning and end of the story rest on the original oracle. Years later, but still long before the play begins, Oedipus in a quarrel killed Laius whom he of course did not recognize. Now the gods have brought a plague on Thebes: they demand discovery and punishment of Laius's murderer. Oedipus piously takes the necessary steps in order that his city, over which he reigns well, may be saved. And the truth is revealed not only that he is the sought-for murderer but that Laius was his father and his wife Jocasta his mother. Oedipus blinds himself and casts himself out of the city.

We are usually taught to see in the story and the play the tragic hero who is brought low. But what was Oedipus's fault? His guilt was objective. That is to say: it existed, first, because he had been destined to it; second, because, in fulfilling his destiny, he murdered his father and married his mother. It existed in several actions, not in his character or his soul, not in the inner motives behind his actions. When Oedipus discovers the truth, he promptly and fully accepts his guilt despite his subjective innocence; he curses his fate not because it was unjust or because he regretted having done what he might have avoided, but because his fate *was* to do terrible things; he curses what he has done and therefore what he is. The divine order is vindicated, as it always is in Sophocles; the end of *Oedipus the King* is that Thebes is saved, and also religion.

Oedipus ends on the note: "Call no man happy until he is dead." Mr Jones comments: We "know nothing in the least" like the "bottomless, relativistic insecurity" of the Sophoclean view.

> There can be no contact between Christianity or in-dividualistic humanism and a cosmic Mutability which averages out rather as the weather does. And because no contact, no experience of Mutability's compensating application to this or that man's singular fate.

For this and similar reasons the refrain runs through the book that Greek drama "remains desperately foreign", "very alien". "Probably not much of the ancient tragic experience is re-coverable by us." The best we can do is to foster "what awareness we can of its near-inaccessibility".

This judgment is ambiguous and seems paradoxical. Certain things are, to be sure, irrevocably lost. We possess only a fraction of fifth-century tragedy, none at all from the fourth century. We have altogether lost the components of music and dance; Mr Jones quite properly reminds us that our approach is therefore "almost bound to be over-literary" and, to that extent, false. Nevertheless, it is not at all obvious in what sense he means that Greek tragedy is nearly inaccessible. In its ideas, its moral considerations and resolutions, just because they are so different from our own? We may not fully comprehend what Aeschylus or Sophocles believed about the workings of the divine order, for example, and we may

find it very alien, but, with Mr Jones's help, do we not comprehend a good deal?

There are, of course, profound epistemological difficulties
surrounding the whole idea of comprehending the past. The
book closes with two sentences from Fustel de Coulanges:
"*Rien dans les temps modernes ne leur [Grèce et Rome] ressemble.
Rien dans l'avenir ne pourra leur ressembler.*" In so far as that is
true, there is no separate problem of the work of art. What
Mr Jones says about tragedy can be said with equal force about
every aspect of life among the ancients. Consider the ties
between 'love', family and status—the latter something
'actual' and not, as with us, 'primarily titular'—which constitute one of Mr Jones's important themes, almost as important as religion in exposing some modern misunderstandings of tragedy and the inaccessibility of the latter. The
complex status structure of classical Greece and Rome, with
chattel slavery at its base, offers no contact with our experience. "Family guilt," writes Mr Jones of the *Oresteia*,
"is as much collective as inherited." And, he continues, the
question "Is he guilty?" has to be purged "of all individual-
istic preconceiving in order to read the answer right" for
both Agamemnon and Orestes. Does he not find such
morality as "desperately foreign" as Greek drama?

There is eminent authority for the view that questions
about the past can be answered, at least approximately,
through the imagination, provided it is disciplined by an
underpinning of sound scholarship. One should, it is held,
be able to share something of the experience of a fifth-century
Athenian audience at a performance of *Oedipus* even though
one does not believe, in the strict sense, in oracles or in the
"divine malice that pervades Greek tragedy". But ideological
differences do not exhaust the difficulties. We read (or see)
Sophocles having read (or seen) Shakespeare, as we look at
archaic Greek sculpture with eyes and minds which have ex-

perienced Michelangelo and Henry Moore. The great tradition is two-directional. As Dr Leavis said of Jane Austen,
"she creates the tradition we see leading down to her. Her
work, like the work of all great creative writers, gives a
meaning to the past." The really crucial problem is whether
we can simply unwind the reel, read Richardson as if Jane
Austen had never written, respond to Orestes or Oedipus as
if there had been no Hamlet.

For the visual arts André Malraux, for one, has answered
with a firm negative: the art of the past survives only as 'myth'.
One may disagree, but it is no longer permissible simply to
ignore the issue and write, as does Professor René Huyghe,
general editor of the Larousse Encyclopaedia of Prehistoric and
Ancient Art: "Man learns to know himself better and to understand his nature . . . from the evidence, direct, irrefutable
and still alive, of his works of art." The absurdity of his
adjectives is immediately apparent from the many different
and contradictory 'understandings' which both periods of art
and individual works have provoked. Nor does it abate the
error to add that the "study of the history of art . . . is subject
to that universal law, the law of development". What is
involved is not a state of mind but the nature of mind. Even
where there is no language barrier (on which too much stress
is often laid), all the complexities of perception and compre-
hension remain.

It is along such lines, I suggest, and not from mere differences
of ideology that Mr Jones can argue most powerfully for near
inaccessibility. But then, when he writes that "it turns out
to be our bad luck that Greek Tragedy is superficially intelligible in a modern way", we part company. There is an
implication here of moral fault, as if preceding generations of
critics and scholars had somehow sinned, even wilfully,
against the tragedians and Aristotle by modernizing them.

No doubt the process was a bad thing in so far as it served

the ends of providing high ancient authority for modern practice. But it was a bad thing because that kind of authoritarianism is bad, and it would have been little better if Aristotle had actually said what he was twisted into saying. Is it bad for Greek tragedy to be "intelligible in a modern way"? Can it be intelligible in any other way? All art is a dialogue. So is all interest in the past. And one of the parties lives and comprehends in a contemporary way, by his very existence. It seems also to be inherent in human existence to turn and return to the past (much as powerful voices may urge us to give it up). The more precisely we listen and the more we become aware of its pastness, even of its near-inaccessibility, the more meaningful the dialogue becomes. In the end, it can be only a dialogue in the present, about the present.

I

THE REDISCOVERY OF CRETE

THE Greek historian Polybius, writing in Rome about 150 B.C., criticized philosophers who included Crete in discussions of the ideal state. "With few exceptions," he said, "you could find no habits prevailing in private life more steeped in treachery than those in Crete, and no public policy more inequitable." Greed and avarice "are native to the soil in Crete", where the people "are engaged in countless public and private seditions, murders, and civil wars".

Polybius had a habit of making sharp and not necessarily reliable generalizations about the people of various Greek regions, especially about those he did not like. Nevertheless, it is true that the Crete of his day was a backwater of the Greek world and a major base for piracy in the eastern Mediterranean. There was nothing very interesting to be studied in the institutions of contemporary Crete. But the island was also a place of legend and traditions, some of them singular and curious. There was, for example, King Minos, who controlled the sea with his navy and was famed for his sense of justice, the gift of his father, Zeus. Minos had at his court that peerless craftsman, the divinely descended Daedalus, a refugee from Athens who made wings with which he and his son Icarus flew away. Icarus soared too close to the sun, his wings melted, and he was drowned in the sea. Minos pursued Daedalus to Sicily and was killed there (also by drowning) by the daughters of a local king, Kokalos. In Hades, on the testimony of Odysseus, who visited the place, Minos could be seen wielding a golden sceptre and dispensing justice.

Myth is rarely consistent, of course, and there was another, less attractive side to Minos. He was married to Pasiphaë, daughter of the Sun, who developed an unnatural passion for a bull that had come out of the sea. Minos himself was in one sense the offspring of a bull, but that was different, for his father was actually Zeus in disguise (his mother was Europa). Pasiphaë, however, was in love with a real bull; she appealed to Daedalus, who rigged up a contraption that enabled her to have intercourse with the animal. Pasiphaë then gave birth to a monster, half man, half bull, called the Minotaur (literally, the Bull of Minos). The king housed the Minotaur in a specially constructed labyrinth and commanded the Athenians, who were his subjects, to supply seven youths and seven maidens every year to be fed to the monster. One year Theseus, the young son of the Athenian king, persuaded his father to include him in the annual consignment of victims. When he arrived in Crete, Theseus promptly won the love of Minos's daughter Ariadne and with her aid slew the Minotaur. The two of them then fled—oddly enough, they were not pursued—but when they reached the island of Naxos, Theseus deserted Ariadne; the god Dionysus found her there and married her.

Zeus's interest in Crete was not restricted to Europa and Minos. He himself was raised on the island, in a cave, where his mother had gone into hiding to save the child from her husband, the Titan Kronos, who had the habit of devouring his offspring. Whether the cave was located on Mount Ida in central Crete or, much more likely, on Mount Dikte farther east, was a matter of dispute. Crete is dotted with mountain caves, and hundreds of them were occupied by neolithic people at least as far back as 6000 B.C. A few became and remained sacred shrines well into the historical Greek period, and conflicting claims were inevitable. But it was agreed by nearly everyone, not just by Cretans, that the island was the motherland of the king of the Olympian gods, and that is of first importance. Why Crete, after all?

There are sites which naturally evoke feelings of mysticism

and awe, which have what students of religion call a numinous quality. Delphi, for example. Visitors to Delphi feel it even today, despite the modern hotels and souvenir shops, the parked cars and tourist buses. Caves and springs have it, too. But it would be difficult to argue that Crete is in any way supremely, or even especially, numinous. It is the largest island in the Aegean Sea, an oblong about 160 miles in length and 36 miles wide at its broadest point, with an area of 3,235 square miles (slightly smaller than Cyprus or, say, Puerto Rico). It is mountainous, and the view when one approaches by sea from the south is harsh, rugged and spectacular. Some parts, notably the White Mountains in the west, are virtually inaccessible, fit only for wild goats and outlaws, today as in antiquity. Once Crete was famous for its cypresses and oaks, its pastoral uplands, its olives and vines, its fertile meadows, its harbours on the northern and eastern sides. (If it is now mostly a barren waste, that is the result of Christian and Saracen mismanagement during and after the Middle Ages.) And it is an island of caves.

Yet when all that is said, the special link of Zeus with Crete remains unexplained, for much the same description can apply with equal truth to many parts of Greece and Asia Minor (modern Turkey), and to other Aegean islands. It was not its geography that gave Crete a special pre-eminence, but its history, or rather, its prehistory. There was a time—between 2000 and 1400 B.C., in round numbers—when Crete had a Golden Age, when it was far richer, more powerful, more civilized, than any other area of what was later to comprise the Greek world. That early culture was destroyed and literally buried: even its physical remains were soon no longer visible. But a vague memory hung on. Life itself did not disappear from the island. Many of the once great centres (though not all), such as Knossos and Gortyn and Phaistos, eventually found a new existence as minor, relatively impoverished Greek cities, dimly aware in a distorted way of a great past, of Minos and his labyrinth and his Minotaur, of being the home of Zeus, the greatest of the Olympian gods.

The dimness of their knowledge must be underscored. If a Cretan in, say, the fifth century B.C. (or any other Greek at that time) were asked about Minos, he would have described him as a great Greek ruler who lived once upon a time. He knew that there had been an age when Crete was inhabited by non-Greeks, whom he called Eteo-Cretans ('true Cretans'), and from whom the people of Praisos in eastern Crete claimed to have descended. But he never doubted that the Golden Age was a *Greek* civilization essentially like his own, only brighter, richer, greater. Did not a grandson of Minos, Idomeneus, lead one of the famous contingents against Troy under Agamemnon? And what were Agamemnon and his Mycenae and the expedition he commanded but Greek, not only in the language they spoke but also in their way of life?

This false image held the field until the beginning of the twentieth century. For most of the intervening centuries few people in western Europe ever gave a thought to Crete, anyway. It was fought over and exploited from time to time by Romans, Byzantine emperors, Saracens, crusaders, Turks, and finally, almost in our own day, by Greeks who brought the island back into the national territory. But it had little intellectual or historical interest, as Polybius already had asserted, whether from reading books or through direct personal investigation.

The first important breakthrough was made in 1834 by a young man from Trinity College, Cambridge, named Robert Pashley. He had completed the normal university course in classics and mathematics, and he was to make his mark at the bar. But first he joined that remarkable con-

stellation of nineteenth-century British explorers and archaeologists—Layard, Burton and Stanley are perhaps the most
famous and certainly the most spectacular—who were opening up vast new and exotic fields of enquiry. At twenty-seven
Pashley had learned from ancient geographers and historians
and from scraps of mediaeval and modern information, some
of it unpublished, everything there was to be known about
the island of Crete. He then set out, accompanied by a Spanish engraver from Malta named Antonio Schranz, to map
and describe as many of the ancient places as he could locate.
He had an Indian scout's eye for terrain, so that a modern
expert could say of his seven-odd months' work that Pashley
"identified most of the important sites with an accuracy
which had never before been attained and has in few cases
since been challenged".

He was also a gifted linguist with a genius for winning the
confidence of the local population, no small reason for his success. Crete in 1834 was still under the rule of the Turks, having
been returned to them in the settlement following the Greek
war of independence of 1821–31. The Cretans, partly Christian, partly Moslem, were illiterate, ignorant and impoverished, and they had no reason to trust anyone. "Before the
outbreaking of the Greek revolution," Pashley wrote, "Crete
was the worst governed province of the Turkish Empire."

Pashley's two-volume illustrated account of his travels was
published in 1837. There were no more volumes, since all
his papers and drawings went up in flames the following year.
What he managed to get into print is fascinating not only for
its detailed explanation of his procedures in making the
identifications he was after but also for its descriptions of
Cretan life, and, incidentally, of what the local population
imagined about their own distant past. One boy of ten, for
example, told him that "the Cretan labyrinth was one of the
seven wonders of the world, in the time of the ancient

Hellenes," and that "these seven wonders correspond to the seven sacraments of the Christian church." Pashley himself had no more idea than the ten-year-old of a great *pre-Greek* civilization. He was looking for Greco-Roman remains and he found some, believing them to belong to "the very earliest period of civilization". When he reached and located Knossos, he was led to remark, as a good rationalist, that the "natural caverns and excavated sepulchres" in the neighbourhood "call to mind the well-known ancient legend respecting the Cretan labyrinth. . . . There is, however, no sufficient reason for believing that the Cretan labyrinth ever had a more real existence than its fabled occupant."

Some seventy years later, Arthur Evans, looking back ten years to his first dig on Crete, was able to write: "The city of Minos, the legendary site of the Palace wrought for him, with all the artistic wonders it contained, by his craftsman Daedalus . . . and of the labyrinth itself, naturally stood out as the first objective." Between Pashley and Evans a complete revolution in thought had occurred—a revolution that was born not on the island itself but first in Asia Minor and then on the mainland of Greece, the achievement of one man, Heinrich Schliemann. Some investigation had been going on in Crete right along, but it stuck, as Pashley had, to Greek remains and Greek documents. The results were by no means unimportant: one find, at Gortyn, comprised large sections of a fifth-century-B.C. law code inscribed on stone, which is still unique among Greek antiquities. The study of Greek history and Greek civilization was thus considerably advanced, while the glory of early Crete remained as hidden and improbable as it had been to Polybius two thousand years before.

Then came the incredible Schliemann—at Troy beginning in 1870, at Mycenae in 1876, and at Orchomenos in central Greece in 1881—and the world learned, to its astonishment, that Greek legends had to be taken seriously after all, even though not as literally as Schliemann himself insisted. Schliemann would not have been Schliemann had he not tried to extend his efforts to Knossos. But there old age and Turkish bureaucratic obscurantism finally thwarted him, and he achieved no more than an unsuccessful trial trench. The secrets of Knossos were left for Evans to discover, and no man has ever dominated an archaeological field so completely (unless it be the Abbé Breuil and prehistoric cave paintings).

Arthur Evans (Sir Arthur from 1911) has unfortunately picked up some legendary qualities in our day, which complicate issues that have since arisen. One is the preposterous notion that he was really a brilliant amateur. The facts are these: son of a distinguished archaeologist and numismatist, he received the best classical and historical education available; he then spent six years at Ragusa (now Dubrovnik) studying the archives and antiquities of the south Slavs and ancient Illyrians. He worked with his father-in-law, the noted historian E. A. Freeman, on the ruins and coins of Sicily, and he had further archaeological experience in Britain. There were very few, if any, better trained archaeologists in all of Europe in 1884, when Evans was appointed Keeper of the Ashmolean Museum in Oxford at the age of thirty-three.

During a visit to Athens, Evans acquired a few engraved sealstones from Crete, on which he thought he detected some signs from an unknown script. Off he went to the island to search for more, which he found without difficulty, for they were being worn by pregnant women as amulets. 'Milkstones,' they called them. In antiquity these stones were also worn round the neck or wrist, but their function was not that of amulets or charms. The engraved design was the owner's stamp or mark, with which he 'sealed' documents or pottery or whatever else required such identification.

The 'milkstones' settled it for Evans: he would dig at

Knossos. Since he was heir to two fortunes, he was able to overcome the difficulties that had stopped Schliemann. In 1894 he bought the site. But he still had to wait until the Turks finally left the island late in 1898, after which he began to excavate almost at once, and in his very first campaign he discovered the palace and a number of inscribed tablets. 'Minoan' civilization, as Evans named it, was reborn in 1900, for he promptly realized that here was a culture far more advanced than that of the Stone Age and at the same time in many of its essential qualities different from the later culture of Athens or Sparta, or even of Greek Knossos. There could be no better or more easily visible symbol of the difference than the great palace itself, the labyrinthine structure which subsequent excavations elsewhere on Crete have shown to be characteristic of the Minoan world. This kind of palace, or any kind for that matter, was totally unknown among the later Greeks. Their characteristic monumental building was the temple framed in columns, a structure that had been wholly unknown to the Minoans. As was monumental sculpture: there were no large statues in Crete, whether of men or of gods. And there were no indications of a supreme male deity: if Zeus was an old god on Crete, and not a later importation, he was a very weak forerunner of the Greek Olympian.

As excavation and study continued, it became obvious that Minoan civilization was palace-centred, with analogies to the contemporary civilizations of the Middle East rather than to later Greece. Behind Minoan civilization lay a very considerable increase in population from the small numbers scattered in the neolithic mountain-cave habitations, a great advance in technology—including the use of metal—and the growth of a complex social organization and power structure. Whoever built the palaces commanded great resources in both materials and manpower, and they had access to ideas and goods from Egypt, Syria and even Babylonia. All the important Cretan centres were near good harbours, or, more accurately, protected beaches, for at this period ships were drawn up on land in bad weather.

Perhaps the most astonishing aspect of this civilization was its apparent peacefulness. The palace complexes were not fortresses like those of Mycenae, Tiryns or other mainland centres. Nor were there traces of any other kind of fortification, and scarcely any of arms and armies. In this respect Crete was utterly unlike its contemporaries. Not even the kings are visible: there is a throne in the throne room at Knossos, but the walls are decorated with mythical animals and floral designs. Control of the seas could explain the feeling of perfect security from attack overseas. But was there never any danger of conflict between palaces? And was there no need for compulsion and police protection at home?

These are obvious questions to ask; they cannot be answered at present because the available evidence consists largely of material objects—buildings, tools, pottery, works of art—and those can never tell us very much about the social institutions or ideas of a civilization. Evans and other archaeologists found numbers of inscribed tablets, but in his lifetime they defied all efforts at decipherment. It is an oddity of Evans's career that, having been drawn to Crete by his discovery of unknown written characters on sealstones, he proceeded to concentrate on everything else he found while neglecting publication of the tablets and probably delaying the decipherment as a result.

Evans died in 1941 at the age of ninety, still at work on his publications. A man of demonic energy and will power, he commanded the loyal support of a group of very able associates, and his pioneering efforts were quickly followed by other excavators all over Crete. He was also a ferocious polemicist who could, and did, crush dissident voices. By 1941, therefore, the generally accepted picture of Minoan Crete was Evans's, including, it is proper to add, no small amount of imaginative inference and reconstruction, as any tourist can see for himself at Knossos today if he is reasonably observant and shuts his ears to the official patter of the guides.

Not that imagination is not an essential tool of the archaeologist. Consider the basic question of dating: when did the Minoan civilization begin, when did it end? Such questions had (and still have) to be answered without the help of a single dated Minoan document. The dating is therefore archaeological—that is to say, it is worked out by careful study of successive layers in the ruins, by marking datable objects imported from other societies, such as Egypt, and observing similarities between them and Cretan objects found in datable contexts elsewhere. To achieve even an approximation of the truth requires great sensitivity to stylistic minutiae and to craftsmanship, which Evans possessed to a very high degree. At best only an approximation will result: it is worth insisting on that just at present, when Cretan chronology is again being debated with a ferocity that is in inverse proportion to the certainty anyone can reasonably claim.

The Evans chronology can be set out in a table (as recently modified by R. W. Hutchinson, who from 1934 to 1947 was Curator of the Villa Ariadne, the headquarters Evans built at Knossos):

Early Minoan	I:	2500–2400 B.C.
	II:	2400–2100
	III:	2100–1950
Middle Minoan	I:	1950–1840 B.C.
	II:	1840–1750
	III:	1750–1550
Late Minoan	I:	1550–1450 B.C.
	II:	1450–1400
	III:	1400–1050

That the pattern is too neatly symmetrical is almost self-evident. It also has an empire-building note to it, for the scheme, worked out from the ruins at Knossos, was imperiously extended to the whole of Crete, though it is now certain that at least some of it will not work at all for other sites, such as Phaistos. And why should it? That the whole of Crete was monolithic in its culture and politics is a gratuitous (and now demonstrably false) assumption. However, once allowance is made for these defects, this is still in broad terms the most generally accepted chronology, with the Middle Minoan recognized as the great creative period and 1400 as the really terminal date. At that time there was massive destruction from which Minoan civilization never recovered. Late Minoan III was dismissed by Evans as a miserable 'squatters' ' world.

After 'when', the next question is, of course, 'who?' That there were migrations into Crete both before and during the Minoan period is beyond doubt. The last of them brought Greeks to the island. But before the Greeks, migrations of whom, from where? These are still fairly open questions to which we shall return shortly. Evans's most famous personal row was over the Greeks. There are unmistakable affinities and influences to be seen between the later Cretan palace art and architecture, and the great civilization then developing on the mainland of Greece (which we call Mycenaean). Evans naturally insisted that the originality and the priority were Cretan, and he nearly succeeded in destroying the career of a younger archaeologist, Alan Wace—eventually the chief authority on Mycenae—who challenged him (and who has since been proved to have been much nearer the truth).

The final verdict, it seemed reasonable to believe, lay locked in the undeciphered scripts, of which more were found than Evans had originally bargained for. When one considers how few different ways of writing man has invented in his entire history, it is astonishing that this small island of Crete should have produced at least two entirely on its own. There was a modified picture writing, which Evans called 'hieroglyphic' on the analogy of the Egyptian script; there were two different, more advanced scripts (in which the individual signs stand for syllables), which he called Linear A and B, respectively; and on a small disk found at Phaistos, possibly an imported object, there was still another system of writing. They are all unique to Crete except Linear B, the use of which was more widespread on the mainland of Greece than in Crete itself, but they occur only in very short texts or in markings on sealstones and pottery, and their brevity adds immeasurably to the difficulties of decipherment. It must be remembered that writing on perishable materials such as Egyptian papyrus—even if there had been any, which we do not know—would not have survived in the Cretan climate. Certain palace records were kept on small leaf-shaped clay tablets that were unbaked and were discarded as soon as they were no longer needed. The destruction of the palaces was accompanied by great conflagrations, which accidentally baked whatever inscribed tablets happened to be on hand, and these alone have been recovered in modern excavations.

In 1952 a young British architect, Michael Ventris, announced after years of intensive work that the language of the tablets written in the Linear B script was an archaic form of Greek. This discovery immediately challenged, though in a tantalizing way, much of what had become the orthodox picture of Minoan civilization. It was now certain that the rulers at Knossos at the time of its destruction were Greek-speaking. But when had they arrived, in what numbers, and with what effect? The tablets carry no dates. Their contents are restricted to the prosaic minutiae of rations, flocks of sheep, inventories of palace goods, and the like. They confirm and elaborate the picture already suggested by the ruins themselves of a very centralized, bureaucratic, palace-run society, but they unfortunately contain no significant information about politics or foreign contacts. And thus far the Linear B script has not been found at any Cretan site other than Knossos. Does this mean that the conquest by speakers of Greek, for such it seems to have been, did not extend to the rest of the island? Perhaps—or perhaps we are being misled by chance, by archaeologists' luck.

Linear B is a script which developed from Linear A, but Ventris's success in reading it has not yet led to the decipherment of the latter. This is partly because the available texts are so few. Although Linear A tablets, unlike Linear B, have been found at a number of Cretan sites, the Linear B fragments from Knossos alone (excluding the mainland in this calculation) outnumber all known Linear A texts by about ten to one. But primarily the block is created by the fact that the language of the Linear A tablets is certainly not Greek and probably not any known tongue. Hard cryptographic work goes on steadily. Occasionally there is a spectacular announcement of a break, but each has proved to be a false alarm, so that it is still correct to say, as John Chadwick wrote in 1958: "we are forced to admit that further progress seems for the moment to be barred by the inadequacy of the material available." One conclusion, however, seems secure: the language of the Linear A script was that of the people who created the Minoan Golden Age, long before a Greek-speaking people came in to rule at Knossos in the final phase; and the syllabic writing was originally invented for that language and later transferred to Greek, to which it was not very well suited (just as cuneiform writing and the Phoenician alphabet were each employed for languages other than the original ones). And so the two old questions still remain unanswered: Who? When?

The tablets cannot answer the second question, not only because they give no dates but also because they are all the product of a single moment in time, the moment when a particular palace was burned. Thus we know that Linear B was in use in Knossos when it was destroyed, but not when the script was introduced there or how much it may have been modified over the years. We must still rely on archaeological dating. Although most archaeologists continue to accept Evans's chronological scheme in essence, at least for Knossos, it is nevertheless being strenuously challenged, chiefly by Professor Leonard Palmer of Oxford. His doubts began from the fact that where Linear B tablets have been found on the mainland, as at Pylos, under the same conditions as at Knossos (again thanks to a conflagration when the palaces were destroyed), the generally accepted date is about 1200 B.C. That is two hundred years later than Evans's date for the end of the great Minoan age, yet the language and general contents of the Knossos tablets are essentially indistinguishable from the mainland ones. The timing, Palmer argues, ought therefore to be about the same. From that simple foundation the argument has become very technical, very complicated, and very acrimonious. Evans's notebooks have been examined to check his published statements against the first impressions jotted down while the digging was going on. New efforts are being made to correlate and synchronize the Knossos remains with those on other sites, where, as has already been said, the neat Evans scheme does not apply except with drastic modifications. And the old, and in the end crucial, question of the precise relations between the two cultures, Cretan and mainland, is being re-argued.

The violence of the polemic has not made it easier for the layman to grasp just what is at issue. One cannot simply shift the destruction at Knossos by two hundred years and leave it at that. If Palmer is right, then the whole chronology of the last great Minoan phase has to be modified, and along with that, our appreciation of the role of the new Greek element, both on the island and on the mainland. If he is right, then perhaps the Linear B script itself was a mainland invention, not a Cretan one. Then, too, Evans's picture of a long miserable squatters' period in Knossos would have to be abandoned, and we should have to think of the great wave of destruction of about 1200 B.C. on the mainland as extending to Crete as well.

To that extent Palmer's dating is an important challenge to the orthodox chronology. On the other hand there is no implication that the total picture of Minoan civilization, from its emergence out of the Neolithic three hundred or more years before 2000 B.C., has to be rejected. More is known today than Evans ever knew, and further knowledge inevitably means correction, elaboration and refinement of the picture. But his achievement stands as one of the great monuments in the history of archaeology, and is all the more remarkable because he began when the subject and its techniques were new and often crude. Any suggestion that Evans was incompetent or dishonest is as preposterous as the myth of his amateurism. It is easy to be clever and superior after someone else has done the back-breaking spadework.

What all parties to the newest dispute do agree on is the integral link between the pre-Greek stratum of the Cretan population and Asia Minor. Some of the evidence is linguistic (and again highly technical), as in pre-Greek place names like Knossos or Tylissos, and some is archaeological. But the most obvious is the omnipresent bull. On Cretan frescoes there are bulls everywhere, in several roles (but never as a deity or anything like the Minotaur, which must be a post-Minoan Greek invention). There are also the mysterious 'horns of consecration', serving sometimes as a base in which the double axe was planted as a sort of standard, the combination possibly having some cult significance. Now the bull is also known in religious contexts from Asia Minor, associated with the Hittite weather-god, for example, and most sensationally in the discoveries made by James Mellaart, beginning in 1961, at Çatal Hüyük in the Konya Plain of south-central Asia Minor. This is a neolithic site, the lowest level of which has been dated 6500 B.C. He found wall paintings not unlike the Stone Age cave paintings of eastern Spain, but also bulls' horns ceremoniously arranged in a way which is remarkably reminiscent of the Cretan 'horns of consecration'.

It is a long jump from Asia Minor in 6500 B.C. to Crete in 2000, but this new find, taken together with all the other known links, cannot be dismissed as meaningless coincidence. The essential point is that these are all links which suggest actual migration from Asia Minor to Crete at some time in the dim past, and not just a borrowing of ideas or institutions, which also went on all the time.

Clearly the rediscovery of Crete is still a very incomplete process. In 1962 the Greek archaeologist Nicholas Platon discovered a great labyrinthine palace, and in 1963 some Linear A tablets, near the village of Kato Zakro on the east coast. This appears to be the fourth largest Cretan palace so far uncovered, after Knossos, Phaistos and Mallia, yet a first-rate archaeologist, Evans's associate D. G. Hogarth, had dug there in 1901 and failed to find it, and no one knows its ancient name. On the mainland of Greece, at Thebes, building operations early in 1964 turned up the first Linear B tablets to be found at that site, along with a number of datable Babylonian sealstones, at least one of them from the period 1375–1350 B.C. The plains of Asia Minor are covered

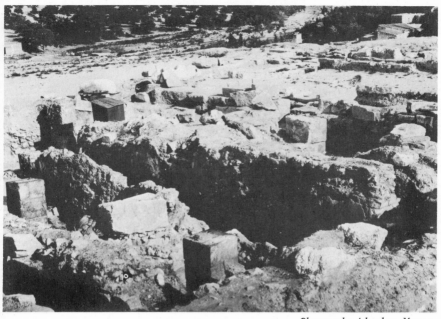

Photograph: Ashmolean Museum

Knossos in 1901: the south part of the west wing, looking southeast.

Knossos today: the northeast corner, seen from the south.

Bildarchiv Foto Marburg

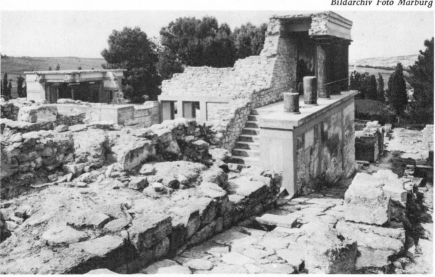

CRETAN SCRIPTS

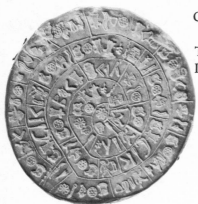

The Phaistos Disk, now in the Iraklion Museum.

Photograph: Ashmolean Museum

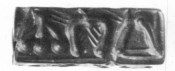

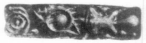

Middle Minoan green jasper 'milkstones' with 'hieroglyph-ic' signs (twice actual size).

Photographs: Ashmolean Museum

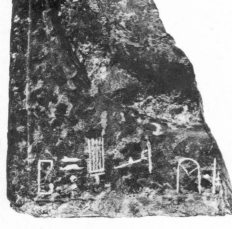

Fragment, lower left-hand cor-ner, of libation table found in Diktaean Cave, inscribed in Linear A.

Photograph: Ashmolean Museum

Linear B tablet from Knossos.

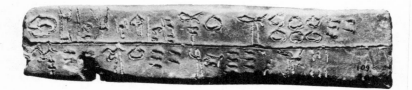

with mounds like Çatal Hüyük, with limitless possibilities. Carbon-14 dating has already pushed the Cretan Neolithic Age back a thousand years, and it may some day provide a scientific answer to the later chronology. Chemical analysis of the clays and pigments of pottery will provide a new and reliable underpinning for stylistic analysis.

It seems inevitable that all these problems and proposals should stir up great dust clouds of publicity, claims and counterclaims being asserted with a certainty and acerbity they do not warrant. The chief harm done in the process is to draw attention away from the essentials to the ephemeral and to personalities. The essential, after all, is a major, in some ways attractive, lost civilization. While we wait for more certain answers to many questions (about origins, connections, dates), the art and the architecture, the technical achievements, the implications about how the society was organized, are there to be contemplated. So is the final catastrophe, whether it occurred in Crete in 1400 B.C. or in 1200 as on the Greek mainland. When the Greeks re-emerged in the full light of history several centuries later, they still spoke Greek, but they wrote in a new script and they had a wholly new way of life. That is why Minoan Crete and Mycenaean Greece are properly part of Greek *prehistory*.

II

LOST: THE TROJAN WAR

THE capture of Troy and the wanderings of Odysseus have had an unrivalled hold on the imagination for more than twenty-five hundred years. The chain of tradition is an unbroken one, through antiquity and the Middle Ages down to our own day, when the word 'odyssey' is a common cliché along with 'Achilles' heel' or 'Trojan horse'. As far back as 500 B.C. or earlier, the Etruscans had a predilection for scenes of the Trojan War on the Greek painted pottery which they imported into central Italy. The Romans then went further and linked themselves directly with the Trojans by fashioning a new foundation legend, incompatible with their older myth of Romulus, from whom the city was supposed to have taken its name. Their new hero-founder was Aeneas, one of the Trojan survivors, and it was around him, not Romulus, that Virgil wrote the great Roman epic, the *Aeneid*. The Roman example later spread, and during the Middle Ages it was commonly believed that English history began with Brute (or Brutus) the Trojan, and that the Franks were descended from Francus, son of Hector.

Our oldest and fullest information about the Trojan War comes from the two poems, the *Iliad* and the *Odyssey*, some sixteen and twelve thousand lines in length, respectively, and both attributed to Homer (though modern scholars on the whole believe in two 'monumental composers', and place them in the eighth century B.C.). Yet they provide nothing like the whole story. The *Iliad* is devoted to a few weeks in the tenth year of the war, ending not with the fall of the city but with the death of Hector, the greatest of the Trojan warriors. The *Odyssey* narrates the wanderings of Odysseus for ten years after the victory, before he could return to his native Ithaca, a small island off the western coast of Greece. There is a good deal of reminiscing, especially in the latter poem, which helps fill out the account, but there are still many missing pieces. For them we depend on fragmentary material scattered throughout Greek and Roman literature of all kinds, such as the great Athenian tragedies, the works of antiquarians and mythographers, or the Latin poems of Ovid. When we try putting all the scraps together, they add up to too many, and often to contradictions. The mythical imagination did not come to an end with the *Iliad* and *Odyssey* but went on creating new variations and combinations as well as reviving old traditions which Homer failed to include.

Inconsistencies arose even about the most central figures. Everyone was agreed, for example, that Helen was the daughter of Zeus and Leda (wife of King Tyndareus of Sparta), but Homer chose to ignore the most interesting and most famous element in the story of her birth. This is how Euripides has Helen herself tell it (in Richmond Lattimore's translation), at the beginning of his tragedy named after her:

> Nor is my own country obscure. It is a place called Sparta, and my father was Tyndareus: though they tell a story about how Zeus took on himself the shape of a flying swan, with eagle in pursuit, and came on wings to Leda my mother, and so won the act of love by treachery. It may be so.

Helen had twin brothers named Castor and Pollux. In the *Iliad* they are mortals (in fact they are already dead), whereas the later Greeks generally believed them to be gods; they were worshipped in Sparta, among the Greek settlers in southern Italy, and elsewhere. Not later than 550 B.C., furthermore, a lyric poet named Stesichorus introduced a radically new twist designed to save Helen's reputation now that moral values had undergone a change. In this version, Paris got Helen as far as Egypt, and there good King Proteus (the Old Man of the Sea) hid her and replaced her with a ghost, whom the addled young Trojan prince took home with him, deluded into thinking that he had the flesh-and-blood Helen.

Such examples can be multiplied a hundredfold. They did not go unnoticed among educated Greeks, and something of a scholarly literature on the subject developed in antiquity. Thus, the great geographer Eratosthenes (who died in 194 B.C.) dismissed as idle the attempts to identify in Sicily and Italy the places where Odysseus had his wondrous experiences —a game which is still being pursued by some modern scholars. "Homer," he wrote, "neither knew them nor wished to set the wanderings in familiar places." Other ancients disapproved of the ethical aspects of the tale, in particular of the Homeric image of the gods. "Homer and Hesiod," protested the philosopher Xenophanes in the sixth century B.C., "have attributed to the gods everything that is disgraceful and blameworthy among men: theft, adultery and deceit." But not one Greek or Roman is on record as having rejected the historical truth of the tale as a whole. Herodotus, the 'father of history', a far more penetrating and far less gullible enquirer than he is often made out to be, ascribed the beginnings of mutual hostility between Greeks and Asiatics to the Trojan War, when "the Greeks, for the sake of a single Spartan girl, collected a vast armament, invaded Asia, and destroyed the kingdom of Priam". In the next generation the still more tough-minded Thucydides introduced and justified his history of the war between Athens and Sparta by arguing that it was the greatest war ever, greater even than the Trojan War. The early Church Fathers, too, had to make allowance for Homer, and an entertaining debate arose between pagans and Christians over the question of priority between Homer and Moses.

In brief outline, the tale they all believed was this. Paris, otherwise called Alexander, one of the sons of King Priam of

Troy (or Ilion), visited Sparta and fell in love with Helen, wife of King Menelaus. His love was returned, thanks to Aphrodite (whom the Romans called Venus), and the pair fled Sparta for Troy, where they lived more or less happily as man and wife. Menelaus, angered by this gross violation of the laws of hospitality, turned for help to his more powerful brother Agamemnon, king of Mycenae. They summoned other Greek princes and chieftains to join in an invasion of Troy, and together they mustered an armada of 1,186 ships in which they set sail from Aulis on the Euripos Strait, between Euboea and the Greek mainland. In the tenth year of the war the Greeks defeated the Trojans and their Asiatic allies; Troy was captured and razed, honour was restored, and some of the returning heroes then entered upon a new series of adventures. While Menelaus and Helen settled down to a peaceful old age in Sparta, Agamemnon was promptly killed by his wife Clytaemnestra (Helen's sister) and her paramour. It was another ten years before the god Poseidon finally allowed Odysseus to see his home again.

The gods played an active part in the story all through, from Aphrodite's initial role in starting it off. Paris had been a favourite of hers ever since the day when, at the command of Zeus, he acted as arbiter and decided for Aphrodite in a beauty contest among three goddesses. The other two, Hera and Athena, were naturally indignant and it was their hatred, especially Hera's, which determined that Troy must fall to the Greeks. It took ten years for this revenge to be consummated, but that was because other gods supported the Trojans in the struggle. Although Zeus himself was apparently reluctant to allow Troy to be destroyed, in the end he was unable to resist the pleas and seductive wiles of his wife Hera.

Whatever the Greeks may have thought of this side of the

story, not an easy question, in modern times it has of course been necessary to disregard it—as poetic licence or allegory or irrelevant pagan superstition—in order to retain the 'human' side as actual history. There are other difficulties as well. There is a scene in the *Iliad*, for example, in which Helen stands with King Priam on the ramparts of Troy and identifies some of the main Greek leaders for him, an odd thing to have to do after ten years. In all those years not a single replacement seems to have been sent to the expeditionary forces, nor does much else seem to have been happening at home. Clytaemnestra took a lover, but otherwise time stood still while everyone waited passively for the war to end.

Stripped of the magic of its poetry and its leisurely pace and richness of detail, the Homeric tale sounds flat and not very credible. But then, one could reduce all great events, whether of legend or of history, to the same empty mediocrity, and that is not my intention. It is precisely the Homeric genius which captured the imagination and which therefore is basically responsible for the way poetry became converted into history. Nor was it only the ancients who accepted the account as true in its essentials, despite the gods and the inconsistencies; so did nearly everyone else down to the nineteenth century.

If we then ask, By what reasoning did intelligent men go on believing for more than 2,500 years that there is historical truth behind the *Iliad* and *Odyssey*, the answer seems to be the one John Milton gave for accepting the legendary history of ancient Britain: "Yet those old and inborn kings, never to have been real persons, or done in their lives at least some part of what so long hath been remembered, cannot be thought without too strict incredulity." Today it will be generally conceded that this is not very powerful reasoning, limited as it is to the single, unpersuasive argument which assigns

28

credibility to a tale just because it has been "so long remembered", that is to say, so often repeated. The rise of modern historical criticism in the nineteenth century destroyed faith in that sort of argument, leading to serious doubts, and then to outright rejection of the historicity of the Trojan War. The English liberal and banker George Grote, whose twelve-volume *History of Greece*, published between 1846 and 1856, was the first major modern work on the subject (and one of the greatest ever written), had no hesitation in calling the whole Trojan story an "interesting fable". Despite its great appeal, he wrote, "it is a mistake to single it out from the rest as if it rested upon a different and more trustworthy basis." There are "two courses, and two only" open to the historian, "either to pass over the myths altogether . . . or else to give an account of them as myths . . . and to abstain from confounding them with ordinary and certifiable history."

The view reflected by Grote was rapidly gaining ground until Schliemann turned the tide with his archaeological discoveries. The latter seized on an idea which was being bruited about that the lost city of Troy lay buried within an 85-foot-high mound called Hissarlik, in the northwestern corner of Turkey, about four miles from the Aegean Sea and dominating a large and fertile plain. He began to dig there in 1870 and at once found fortification walls. Soon he produced incontrovertible proof that Hissarlik had been an important citadel with a long history, unearthing, among other things, weapons, jewellery, and gold and silver objects.

Six years later Schliemann turned his attention to Mycenae in Greece, and within a few weeks again struck gold—literally—when he uncovered the so-called Shaft Graves with their remarkable treasures. In his mind that was double proof, material proof, of the Homeric tales; that was the 'independent evidence', the lack of which men like Grote had made so much of. In the ensuing decades Schliemann's arguments, supported by further archaeological discoveries, won over just about everyone. It can no longer be seriously doubted that Hissarlik is the Troy of legend and history, even to such details as the masses of horse bones found there. "Thus they performed the funeral rites for Hector, tamer of horses" is the final line of the *Iliad*. Nor can it any longer be doubted that many of the places in Greece (though not all) named in the Homeric poems as the seats of power were in fact important centres in the period when the Trojan War supposedly took place.

However, it is necessary to be equally clear about what archaeology has not substantiated. The Homeric description of the site of Troy is sufficiently unlike the actual site to warrant the verdict of Professor Rhys Carpenter of Bryn Mawr, who wrote in 1946 that "there is something wrong either with Schliemann's Troy or with Homer's". Nor did the mainland Greek coalition (or anyone else) level Troy to the ground once and for all: the site was reoccupied and the ruins rebuilt after each of several destructions. To be sure, these are not decisive objections, and they can legitimately be attributed to the inaccuracies and exaggerations inevitable in the transmission of a tale by word of mouth for many centuries. But the difficulties with the date of the war are more serious. The two great 'treasures' that Schliemann found, at Troy and at Mycenae, belong to the wrong civilizations. The war which lay at the core of the tradition could not have occurred at the time when either of the two 'treasures' was deposited. The Trojan one falls in the era which archaeologists now call Troy II, 2500–2200 B.C., before there were any Greeks in Europe at all and about a thousand years before the Mycenaean age in Greece. And the Shaft Grave treasure of Mycenae is also too early, being dated before 1500 B.C. The next flourishing period in Trojan history, its mightiest to judge from the fortifications, is Troy VI, which lasted from about 1800 to about 1300 B.C., the period when the horse made its appearance in that part of the world. Troy VI also ended in massive destruction, not only at the wrong time again but, worse still, apparently as the result of earthquake rather than of human agency, if the ruins have been correctly interpreted.

Troy VI was immediately followed by a shabby, impoverished community huddled in one small sector of the ridge, as unlike the Homeric picture of the large and wealthy city of Priam as one could imagine. That city, Troy VIIa, was also destroyed, and it—if any—unfortunately has to be the city of the Trojan War. At least it had links with mainland Greece, as shown by the Mycenaean potsherds found by the excavators, and the date of destruction—the guesses range between about 1260 and 1200 B.C.—does fall within the right century, the age of the big palace centres in Greece. Nothing has been found, however—and it is necessary to stress that 'nothing' is to be understood literally, not a single scrap—that points to *who* the destroyers were. In other words Trojan archaeology has not been able to substantiate the Homeric tales on this most essential point despite repeated assertions by archaeologists to the contrary.

What about Mycenaean archaeology, then? Troy has not produced a single written text, in any language, but we can now read the clay tablets, written in the script conventionally called Linear B, found at Mycenae and Pylos in Greece (and a few at Thebes in 1964), as well as at Knossos in Crete. What do they contribute to a solution of the puzzle? The plain answer is that they, too, have not come up with a single scrap of information which points explicitly to Troy or a Trojan War, or even so much as mentions Troy. The best that can be squeezed out of all our new knowledge of this period in Greece is a number of statements beginning 'if there really was a Trojan War'—then Mycenae and Pylos and other centres named in the *Iliad* were strong enough in the century from 1300 to 1200 B.C. to assemble a considerable invasion force, and they had contacts with various places on the Turkish coast, and they might have joined in a coalition. But these are all 'might have beens' and no more.

Our only ground for thinking that there was a Trojan War remains the old tradition, and the motives for such a complicated overseas expedition still have to be explained. Herodotus may have believed that the abduction of Helen was reason enough, but no serious historian today is prepared to rest his acceptance of the war on such a paltry excuse, romantic though it may be. And no acceptable alternatives come to mind naturally. The pottery reveals continuous trading relations not only with Troy but also with other Levantine regions, and there is nothing to suggest a trade war. If one imagines a raid for booty, the objections are, first, that the war we are told about is wildly out of scale, even allowing for poetic exaggeration; second, that the raiders made a terrible mistake in going after a miserable place like Troy VIIa when there were any number of more profitable possibilities, and that they can be assumed to have known enough about the whole area to have avoided so preposterous an error.

One further source of information needs to be explored. In precisely the two centuries we call the Mycenaean age, the fourteenth and thirteenth, the Hittites controlled a considerable empire, which embraced most of present-day Turkey, made its influence felt in Syria, and dealt on a level of equality with Egypt and Assyria. The royal archives of the Hittites, discovered in 1907 at Boghaz-Köy in central Turkey, include thousands of official documents of the kind that the Linear B tablets of Greece have failed to produce: laws, decrees and treaties. Perhaps twenty texts, most of them unfortunately in a fragmentary condition, mention a kingdom or territory called Achchijawa, which was independent, usually on more or less friendly terms with the Hittites, but lesser in size and power. Once a sick Hittite king summons the gods of Achchijawa in his search for a cure; another time an enemy is banished to Achchijawa; still another time, when the Hittites are at war with Assyria, the Hittite king orders that "no ship shall sail there from the land of Achchijawa".

The relevance of all this lies in the probability that 'Achchijawa' is the Hittite form of the Greek 'Achaea'. The Homeric poems employ three different names for the Greeks, the most common of which is 'Achaeans'. If, therefore, the identification Achchijawa-Achaea is correct—the philological argument is complicated and not all experts are satisfied—then the Hittite texts confirm the authenticity of the Homeric tradition on one important point, since 'Achaean' ceased to be a generic name for the Greeks in later times.

Again trouble follows at once. Where was Achchijawa located? The Hittite documents offer no satisfactory clues, but imply that Achchijawa, like the other territories mentioned, somehow adjoined Hittite territory. That would exclude the Greek peninsula, though a few historians still try to place Achchijawa there. The island of Rhodes is one plausible suggestion, and there is archaeological evidence of Mycenaean activity on the island in this period. Be that as it may, the great disappointment is that nothing points to Troy. Barring one possible and uninformative exception, Troy is never mentioned, at least not in any recognizable form, in a Hittite document, whether in connection with Achchijawa or in any other context. There is no archaeological evidence of trade or even influence from the Hittites to Troy or vice versa. The Hittite sphere apparently stopped short of the north-western corner of Turkey. And thus, whatever the truth about Achchijawa, no direct light is shed on Graeco-Trojan relations in general or on the Trojan War in particular. Nor did the Hittites make any impact on the Greek tradition; there is not a trace of them in the Homeric poems or in any of the other bits of the composite legend that have survived.

The documents of the last decades of the thirteenth century reveal that the Hittite empire was in trouble. By 1200 or 1190 it was destroyed. No text tells us who accomplished that, but we now have a pretty good idea of what was going on. By 1200 or 1190 Troy VIIa, too, had fallen; so had most of the great fortresses in Greece and important local states in northern Syria such as Ugarit (modern Ras Shamra) and Alalakh; there was turbulence in the west, in Italy, Sicily and Libya; there were repercussions as far east as Babylonia and Assyria. All this did not happen at once, but it was concentrated within a few decades. It would be going too far, on present evidence, to suggest a single unified operation, but there is a case for thinking that the main impulse was a massive penetration by migrating invaders from the north, similar in scale, procedure, and effects to the later Germanic migrations into the Roman Empire.

These invaders sometimes appear in modern writings under a misleading name, 'Sea Peoples', thanks to a careless reading of two important Egyptian documents. The first records how, about 1220 B.C., Pharaoh Merneptah staved off an attack in the Nile delta by the king of Libya and 'Sea People' mercenaries. The second and more important is an account of the successful resistance by Pharaoh Ramses III of a full-scale land and sea invasion through Syria in about 1190. Neither text actually says 'Sea Peoples'; they imply that the invaders came from across the sea, and the earlier one is quite specific: "northerners coming from all lands". Various names are listed, but identification is very speculative except for the Peleset of the Ramses engagement, who were surely the Philistines. Presumably they turned north after their defeat and settled on the Palestinian coast, where we find them in the Old Testament period. One of the groups in the 1220 raid is called Akawash, and it is tempting to see Achaeans again, this time lurking behind an Egyptian variant of the name. The difficulty is that the Akawash are described as circumcised, a fact which the Pharaoh mentions on his victory monument because the consequence was to deprive him of his favourite trophy, the foreskins of vanquished enemies. The Greeks, of historical times at least, did not practice circumcision.

The Greek tradition knew nothing about the 'Sea Peoples' and the damage they wreaked from Italy to Asia. It did not 'remember' the wholesale destruction of the Mycenaean centres, nor even that there had been a Mycenaean civilization which came to an end about 1200 B.C., to be replaced by a new kind of society that was eventually to become their own. For the later Greeks, Agamemnon and Odysseus and Achilles were essentially Greeks like themselves. They were, however, more heroic and at the same time more primitive, and that is why they could be permitted to organize an otherwise incredibly massive expedition "for the sake of a single Spartan girl".

The historical problem we are now presented with is whether the great destructive wave culminating in the eastern Aegean about 1200 or 1190 provides the correct context within which to place and explain the archaeologically proved disaster that befell Troy VIIa at this time—an alternative context to the traditional one. Since an affirmative answer seems plausible, there is nothing to prevent us from going further and suggesting that there may have been Achaean participants. In so greatly disturbed a period it would hardly be surprising if the invading migrants found some friends, allies and fellow freebooters as they swept through Greece.

But plausibility is not enough. The great majority of scholars still prefer to hold to the tradition, at least to its core.

The *Iliad* and *Odyssey*, it is pointed out, are the greatest examples of heroic poetry, a genre known in many parts of the world. Heroic poetry is composed orally, the work of illiterate but highly skilled and professional bards who are able to transmit long and complicated tales from generation to generation. The mediaeval Grand Prince Vladimir of Kiev was still being sung about in the twentieth century, as was the battle of Kosovo at which the Ottoman Turks administered a shattering defeat to the Serbs in 1389. And the twentieth-century poems contain an element of historical truth on both themes. Therefore, the argument goes, the *Iliad* and *Odyssey*, composed with a genius which the Slavic bards cannot approach, must also have a large historical kernel, and even a much more considerable one.

The Homeric poems have been proved to be right on the name 'Achaean' and on some of the geography of the Mycenaean world; by this reasoning they must also be right about the coalition war and the leadership of Agamemnon. Perhaps. But if the Serbian bards could invent the main hero at the battle of Kosovo, and if the French *Song of Roland* can get the enemy wrong, and if the German *Nibelungenlied* can get just about everything wrong; if the Homeric poems contradict most of what we know about the actual working of Mycenaean society, and if their Troy, though in the right place, bears little resemblance to the archaeologists' Troy, and if they are unable to provide a reasonable explanation for the war or a reasonable account of it—then how can one tell what bits, if any, are historical? Without further evidence the debate thus tends to reduce itself to affirmation and denial of John Milton's dogma: the historicity of the Trojan War either can or cannot "be thought without too much strict incredulity".

Always we come back to the genius of the *Iliad* and the *Odyssey*. We no longer read the *Aeneid* or *King Lear* as true stories, as men once did. We certainly do not try to write mediaeval French history from the *Song of Roland* or mediaeval German history from the *Nibelungenlied*. Why should we make an exception of Homer's Trojan War?

III

SILVER TONGUE

IN May 1937 Ezra Pound wrote to W. H. D. Rouse:

No, I will *not* help you reinflate Pindar. . . . Call me bdy. barbarian. I do *not* believe Pindar was the 67th part of Homer. All right in dilettantism for a bloke that knew Homer backwards by heart.

And already twenty years earlier: "a damn'd rhetorician half the time", "the prize wind-bag of all ages". These are hard words about the only Greek lyric poet whose work has survived in some completeness, one whose admirers are as diverse as Horace, the early Pléiade and Goethe.

Yet one sees what annoys Pound. Whatever Pindar's popularity may have been in his own day, ever since he has been either a poet's poet or a scholar's poet. For the former he is the eponym of the high style: a literary language in the narrow sense, flooded with imagery in great bursts, at times defying logic and syntax, intense and subtly, if melodramatically, rhythmic—a master or a wind-bag according to taste. For the scholar he is a bottomless reservoir of mythical allusions, gnomic epigrams and contemporary morals and politics, requiring identification and learned commentary. The Pindar industry began fairly early in antiquity, as we still see in the surviving scholia: it carried on in the Byzantine East during the Middle Ages, and it still goes on. Of course, all major poets have been subjected to the 'How Many Children Had Lady Macbeth' treatment. But whereas Horace or Shakespeare can be read and enjoyed in blissful indifference to the industry, it is at least arguable that Pindar cannot. He is more untranslatable than most and he demands a high standard of Greek to be read in the original. He is also unintelligible, more often than not, without explication. That

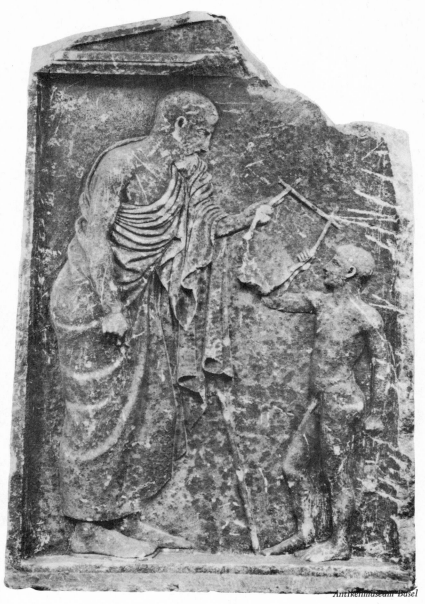

Marble tombstone (about 37 by 26 inches) of a lyric poet from Boeotia, contemporary with the death of Pindar.

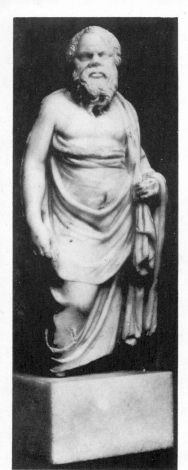

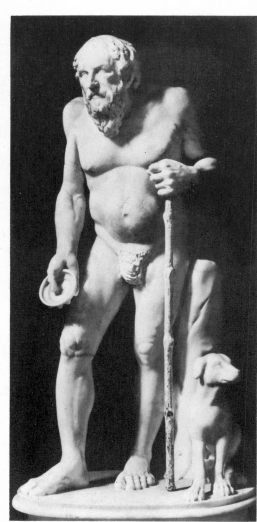

Socrates: marble (about 11 inches high) found in Alexandria, perhaps a second-century-A.D. copy of a second-century-B.C. original.

British Museum

Figure of Diogenes: marble (about 21 inches high), heavily restored, now in the Villa Albani.

Photograph: Mansell Collection

is the warrant for the scale, erudition and earnestness of Sir Maurice Bowra's important effort at 'reinflation' in his *Pindar*.*

In the course of his long life (the probable dates are 518–438 B.C.), Pindar wrote a large number of poems for a variety of purposes and occasions. Of these we have 45 in full, nearly all of them odes in honour of victors in the sporting contests at the great games. They were written on commission to be sung chorally at a victory celebration. We know nothing about the music, but it is fair to judge them solely as literary works, for that is how they circulated even in his own day. They range in length from very short poems to the Fourth Pythian, twelve and a half pages in Richmond Lattimore's translation. Their formal structure is carefully worked out; the technical skill is of the highest order; the professionalism is revealed immediately by the fact that "no extant complete poem is built on precisely the same metrical plan as any other".

I mean professionalism here in all its connotations. Pindar was the greatest of a class of men at that particular period in Greek history who made a career of poetry and who made no bones about writing for money.

> *Muse, you have made a bargain to hire*
> *Your tongue for silver*
> *And have got to keep it agog, now here, now there . . .*

No doubt the Homeric bards were equally professional, but in Pindar and his colleagues—competitors, rather—we have the first proper case-study of the commissioned artist and his patron, and the analogy with the painters and sculptors of the Renaissance is often striking. There is the same rivalry, easily becoming angry and nasty. In 468 Hiero, tyrant of Syracuse, finally won the greatest of all the contests, the chariot race at

* (London and New York: Oxford University Press, 1964).

Olympia. Pindar had reason to expect the commission for the victory ode, but it went instead to Bacchylides. The angry Pindar then composed his so-called Second Pythian, a poetic epistle, full of indignation, self-pity and resignation.

> But I must keep from the sharp bites of slander:
> For far in the past I see
> Archilochus the scold in poverty
> Fattening his leanness with hate and heavy words.

Pindar was at the top of his profession. Hence he could permit himself liberties and a measure of 'independence'. He is constantly calling attention to himself and his prophetic mission.

> To be her chosen
> Messenger of wise words
> To the fine dancing-places of Hellas
> The Muse has raised me up.

He gives advice freely (though no advice could have been more welcome to the recipients and therefore good for the donor). But he never forgets that he is the hireling of powerful, capricious and pitiless men, who will treat him as badly as Hiero did and who can reduce him to the sad fate of Archilochus of old, "the scold in poverty". More than 2,000 years before Brecht, Pindar knew it was a crime (but not yet the greatest) not to have money. It is hard on occasion to resist the word 'toady', but Sir Maurice, too kind and excusing, manages to do so.

The one choice Pindar did not have if he was to continue in his profession was in his patrons. The tyrants of Sicily and of Cyrene in North Africa, the traditional aristocracies of Aegina, of his native Thebes, even of Athens—they and their protégés dominated the sporting events at the games, and it was their world and their values which Pindar celebrated, and obviously shared. His poetry therefore raises, within limits, the question which still exercises critics of T. S. Eliot. Can one divorce a great poet from his deeply felt but odious beliefs?

Our difficulty is made more acute by the fact that an older contemporary of Pindar's, Simonides, who died in 468 B.C. aged nearly ninety, was able to escape total commitment to tyranny and horsy aristocracy. Relatively little of Simonides survives, but that little includes a famous epigram on the dead at Marathon, whereas the sole reference to Marathon in Pindar is as the seat of unimportant local games. Not only did Pindar's native Thebes fail to support the effort to throw back the Persian invasions but Thebans actually fought in the invading army. Sir Maurice notes that the pro-Persian element in Thebes was "the class to which Pindar himself belonged", but he then tries hard to extricate Pindar from his equivocations on the subject. I do not think it can be done. Nor, when Pindar is impressed with Arcesilas of Cyrene as a "king in the heroic manner", does that reflect anything more than a courtier's stance. The poet allows his respect for Arcesilas's position to "spread to the man who holds it". That is the essence: whatever Pindar touches—and that means the inherent rightness of rule by kings, tyrants and nobles and the inherent truth of the myths which he knows so well and which he weaves so skillfully into his praises—he accepts without probing or doubting. What has been and has been believed is right.

One must not be misled by Pindar's admonitions of virtue, justice and the rule of law. He means them in their archaic or Spartan connotations, as they were being bandied about by every oligarch against the growing demand for popular government and democratic rule. It has been pointed out that the "quieter moral virtues" are absent in his ethics. Daring, strength and success are what matter, and behind them the wealth without which none of the requisite activity is possible. There is no glory in defeat, no consolation for the defeated.

> *And now four times you came down with bodies beneath you,*
> *—You meant them harm—*
> *To whom the Pythian feast has given*
> *No glad homecoming like yours.*
> *They, when they meet their mothers,*
> *Have no sweet laughter around them, moving delight.*
> *In back streets, out of their enemies' way,*
> *They cower; for disaster has bitten them.*

These were value-judgments still widely shared by Greeks of his day. One could not possibly say of Pindar's contemporaries, as Professor Kermode wrote of Eliot's, that "it is doubtful whether many have much sympathy now with his views". Pindar lived at a time of conflict and uncertainty. His athletes were still everyman's heroes, but their class and their class-values were being challenged. Even Aeschylus, who is regularly bracketed with Pindar in modern accounts, worried about the implications of the received myths. Hence the *Oresteia* is a serious, if ultimately unresolved, discussion of an ancient moral dilemma. There are no such discussions in Pindar; there are not even any dilemmas, only successes and failures.

The contrast with Simonides is particularly revealing. As Sir Maurice wrote in his *Greek Lyric Poetry*,*

in poetry Simonides stood for more old-fashioned methods than Pindar. . . . But in Athens he learned something more. He moved in the same world as Aeschylus, and was sincere and serious in a time of enormous changes, which he observed and understood in the amplitude of their possibilities.

* (London and New York: Oxford University Press, rev. ed. 1961).

But from Pindar we get neither understanding nor even a clear awareness that new impulses are in the air for him to resist, only an occasional

> *Wise is he who knows much by nature;*
> *Mere learners babble loudly. . . .*

Philosophers and scientists "pick an unripe fruit of wisdom". Poetry may be near to prophecy, but no one reading Pindar would guess that poetry, too, had its place at the great festivals, and not just boxing, wrestling and racing on foot or in chariots.

IV

THUCYDIDES THE MORALIST

NORMALLY the fame of ancient wars is fashioned by myth and romance. Helen of Troy, the Pass of Thermopylae, Alexander, Hannibal—these are the people and the incidents that keep wars alive. But not so the Peloponnesian War, fought between Athens and Sparta from 431 to 404 B.C. (with a seven-year break in the middle). It lives on not so much for anything that happened or because of any of the participants, except for Alcibiades in a minor key, but because of the man who wrote its history, Thucydides the Athenian. No other historian can match this achievement; no other war, or for that matter no other historical subject, is so much the product of its reporter.

That is achievement enough. It becomes even greater when we look more closely at the man and his book. All that we know about Thucydides is found in the few scraps he tells us himself and in a short, eccentric and unreliable biography from late antiquity credited to someone named Marcellinus. But clearly he was a humourless, not very lovable man—pessimistic, sceptical, highly intelligent, superficially cold and reserved, but with strong inner tensions which occasionally broke through the impersonal tone of his writing in savage whiplash comments. He wrote in a complicated style, overloaded and lacking in charm. He refused to make the slightest concession to his audience, whether in style or in treatment of the subject. Nothing mattered but the events and the issues; these he would get right by persistent devotion to accuracy and understanding, and he would report his findings plain. Let the reader who wants romance go elsewhere, he says, I am not writing for the applause of the moment, but for all time.

He was a young man, probably in his late twenties, when the war began. Immediately, he perceived that this would be war on an unprecedented scale, and he decided to become its historian. How he went about his self-assigned task we do not know, for he says very little about his methods apart from a famous brief passage on the unreliability of eyewitness testimony. My narrative, he writes, "rests both on what I saw myself and on the reports of others, after careful research aiming at the greatest possible accuracy in each case. . . . My conclusions have been reached with effort because eye-witnesses disagree about the same occurrence, from imperfect memory or from bias." He never names his informants, and on only two occasions does he say that he was a direct partici-pant. It is left to us to conjure up a picture of Thucydides seeking out a vast number of witnesses from both sides, cross-questioning them closely, deciding on their veracity, piling up notes, sorting out the data, selecting and thinking and writing. He read whatever there was to be read, but that would have been very little, for this was a world of talk, not of writing. Basically, everything—the debates in the as-sembly, the embassies, the behind-the-scenes manoeuvres, the battles—had to be reconstructed from what he was told or had witnessed.

As an able-bodied Athenian citizen, Thucydides was of course not free to give all his time to his project. This was a war in which everyone was mobilized. But in 424 he was exiled on a charge of failure to carry out properly an assign-ment as commander in the north-east. It is characteristic of him that he reports this fact briefly and without comment, except to add that he was in a better position thereafter to obtain information from both sides. His paternal ancestors had connections in Thrace and he retained property there, which enabled him to go on with his work at leisure. He lived through the entire war, was apparently permitted to return to Athens when it ended, and died not many years later.

When he died, someone (his daughter, one tradition has it) published the manuscript exactly as he left it, and there are some very puzzling aspects about the shape of the work at that stage. The whole of the last book is utterly unlike the preceding seven: it has the look of a collection of notes, organized but not worked up. It breaks off abruptly in the year 411 B.C., nearly seven years before the war ended. One might reasonably surmise that Thucydides had stopped writing when he reached that point in his story. However, there are substantial portions early in the volume that could not have been written until after 404, such as the discussion of the exact dating of the war and its duration. Thucydides was obviously working away at his *History* long after 411. But instead of continuing with the narrative, he revised and refashioned some of the earlier parts, and he wrote long chunks in them for the first time. There can be little doubt, for example, that both the Funeral Oration, which Pericles is said to have delivered in the first year of the war, and his last speech, in 430, were written by Thucydides not contemporaneously but nearly thirty years later. They are the old historian's retrospective views of the strength and great possibilities of Athens when the war began, written in the light of his city's complete, and unnecessary, defeat. And even earlier, in the first book with its detailed account of the incidents leading up to the war, there are some sentences that look very much like marginal notes Thucydides had made for himself, for still further recasting and rewriting.

We shall never know what was going on in Thucydides' mind in those final years; what it was that drove him back to the earlier years at the cost of a complete neglect of the ending. It is necessary to make some sort of reasonable guess, however, in order to get at his thinking in general. There is not a sentence in the book that states explicitly what Thucydides thought history was about, why it was important to write an accurate history of the war, or why that history would be a "possession for all time". These were far from obvious questions in his day, for the simple reason that the writing of history had scarcely begun. The Greeks were deeply attached to their past, but it was the distant past, the age of heroes, which attracted them and which they never tired of learning about from Homer and the tragic poets. For the rest, popular traditions served well enough—the stories about Solon and the tyrants and a handful of other figures. No doubt these stories were not very accurate, but what did that matter? Myths and half-truths performed the two necessary functions: they gave the Greeks a feeling of continuity, of nationhood, and they were the source of religious and moral teaching. Neither of these purposes required precise chronology, accurate detail, or complete documentation. In short, there seemed to be no need for history as the modern world understands it, or as Thucydides understood it.

To be sure, there were sceptics and rationalists who were dissatisfied. They neither believed in the philandering of Zeus and the crookedness of Hermes nor approved of a moral code with so unreliable a foundation. By Thucydides' time a considerable line of philosophers had been challenging the whole mythical structure and developing newer and more advanced systems of metaphysics and ethics on rational bases. However, it was not from such concerns that the impulse came for the writing of history, but from the political situation of fifth-century Greece. Herodotus was born and brought up in Halicarnassus, across the Aegean Sea from Athens, in that part of the Greek world which was in closest contact with the 'barbarians', and which for many years had been subject to the Persians and before them to the Lydians.

There a body of writing had grown up consisting of descriptions of manners and customs, geography, and fragments of history. Herodotus apparently planned another such work and travelled very widely collecting the necessary information. But then he came to Athens, was completely enthralled by it, and was inspired to an altogether new vision of his vocation. A generation earlier the Persians had mounted two great invasions of the Greek mainland, and had been driven back, heavily defeated, against all the odds, thanks largely to the moral and practical leadership given by the Athenians. This was a heroic tale as worthy as that of the Trojan War, and it would soon be lost from memory unless it were fixed in writing. And so Herodotus wrote the first book about Greek history.

Thucydides read it and was tremendously impressed. He saw, as virtually no other contemporary saw, that Herodotus had made a very great discovery—namely, that it was possible to analyze the political and moral issues of the time by a close study of events, of the concrete day-to-day experiences of society, thereby avoiding the abstraction of the philosophers on the one hand and the myths of the poets on the other. He saw, too, that the struggle between Athens and Sparta had something of the epic quality of the Persian Wars and was equally profound in its meaning and its consequences. It was worth the whole of a man's life, he thought, to master the unfolding events in all their detail, their complexity, and their deepest meanings.

Thucydides began with an enormous advantage over Herodotus. The latter had had to re-create, for the most part, the atmosphere and the events of a period long past (though some of the battles between the Greeks and the Persians took place when he was a boy). whereas Thucydides was a contemporary and an actual participant. He then set himself a standard of accuracy which, commonplace as it may seem today, was quite extraordinary in the fifth century B.C. "So few pains," he complained, "do most men take in the inquiry for the truth, preferring to accept the first story that comes to hand." The only possible models were among a few philosophers and among the medical writers of the school of Hippocrates, then at its height on the island of Cos. But the mere existence of parallels will not explain why Thucydides transferred their passion for accuracy to the field of history. Like all such personal matters, the question defies explanation. Whatever the reason, it left him an exceedingly lonely figure in the history of ancient historical writing, for not one man after him, among either the Greek historians or the Roman, shared his passion. In this sense, Thucydides' kind of history was a dead-end street. Only among a few scientists, Aristotle and his disciples, for example, do we find anything comparable, and they never took history seriously.

From the beginning, too, Thucydides took still another extraordinary step. Human history, he decided, was a strictly human affair, capable of analysis and understanding entirely in terms of known patterns of human behaviour, without the intervention of the supernatural. It is impossible to say what his religious beliefs were, except that he detested the soothsayers and oracle-mongers who were a plague in wartime Athens. As a historian he recognized their existence in several brief, utterly contemptuous remarks. Otherwise, apart from a few not easily explained references to Fortune (*Tyche*), his *History* unfolds without gods or oracles or omens. Again the Hippocratic writings are the only parallel, and on this score it is scarcely credible that the lives of Herodotus and Thucydides overlapped.

49

These were matters of fundamental outlook, and they gave Thucydides' work its tone. But they could not provide the techniques. How does one go about writing the history of a long war? Thucydides had no precedent to fall back on, no book, no teacher from whom he could learn the business of being a historian. Not even Herodotus, for he was too diffuse, interested in too many things, while Thucydides proposed to concentrate very narrowly on the war and its politics. Apart from everything else, this difference in scale and intensity made Herodotus an unsatisfactory model.

Consider something as elementary as dates. We say that the Peloponnesian War began in 431 B.C. An Athenian had to say that it began in the archonship of Pythodorus, which was meaningless to a non-Athenian, and indeed even to Athenians twenty or thirty years later, unless they had a list of the archons (who held office for only one year) before them while they read. In a large-scale war, furthermore, with many things happening in different places at the same time, dating by years alone would not give the right kind of picture for Thucydides. All the little connections and sequences, the day-to-day causes and consequences, would be lost. Introducing months would not help. Every city had its own calendar: the names of the months were not all alike, nor was the order, nor even the time of the new year. To write a coherent narrative, therefore, Thucydides had to invent a system. After fixing the beginning of the war, he dated all subsequent events first by counting the number of years that elapsed from the start, and then by dividing each war year into halves, which he labelled summer and winter. Simple enough, yet the scheme was unique and the difficulties in making it work are nearly unimaginable today.

Fixing the beginning was almost the hardest problem of all. Wars do not erupt out of nothing on one particular day. The first shot or the formal declaration of war can conveniently be called the beginning of a war, but cannot be the beginning of its history. How far back must the historian go? That is a most critical decision for him; on it depends the interpretation he presents to his readers. In the two decades between 1919 and 1939, three radically different views of the causes of the First World War prevailed, in turn, among students of modern history. Each required its own account of the prehistory of the war. Likewise, in late fifth-century Athens there were sharp disagreements about the causes of the Peloponnesian War, and there were, no doubt, similarly conflicting views elsewhere in the Greek world.

Thucydides sorted out the essential from the casual, the primary causes from the more immediate grievances and the pretexts. The latter he wrote up in very great detail, devoting the whole of the first book to the background. The result is clear, brilliant, and yet somehow unsatisfactory. Thucydides himself was never satisfied with it. Ideas which seemed right early in the war lost their persuasiveness twenty or twenty-five years later. From that distance in time the grievances of Corinth over Corcyra and Potidaea, for example, no longer loomed so large. The Athenian empire had a different look, even retrospectively, after it was broken apart; so did Pericles, after a succession of leaders like Cleon and Hyperbolus, for whom Thucydides felt a contempt and an anger that he does not disguise. More and more it was pure politics, power against power, the rights and wrongs, the morality of power, which seemed the only important and permanent elements in the picture, with the concrete details mere exemplifications. "The truest cause," he came to believe, was this: "The growth of the power of Athens and the alarm which it inspired in Sparta made war inevitable."

Sorting out, selecting what goes into and what is to be excluded from the mass of available data, highlighting and underscoring—these are of course what the historian, any historian, does all the time. Consciously or not, he is applying his personal canons of relevance, and that means his ideas about the nature of politics, of social behaviour, in a word, about history. Even when a historian is explicit and tells us what he thinks history is about, he is judged not so much by his theoretical remarks as by the work itself. Thucydides tells us nothing, so that only the work in the form in which he left it reveals his thinking. And the work is, in a sense, self-contradictory; the historian seems to be pulling, and to be pulled, in opposite directions all the time.

On the one hand, there is a passion for the most minute detail: minor commanders, battle alignments, bits of geography and the like, so that a mere index of names occupies thirty-two double-column small octavo pages. On the other hand, there are astonishing gaps and silences, whole chunks of history that are left out altogether or dismissed in a phrase or odd sentence. For example, there is a marvellous account of the brutal civil war between the oligarchic and democratic factions in Corcyra in 427 B.C., but scarcely a mention of other such struggles (until the oligarchic coup in Athens in the year 411). Yet it is obvious that internal faction played an important part all through the history of the war, and Thucydides himself knew it and stressed it. Then there is the famous contradiction between the narrative, to which he applies all his powers and discipline in the search for total accuracy, and the speeches, in which he brings out the central issues and conflicts *as he saw them*—but not necessarily as the speakers saw them, and surely not exactly as the speakers expressed them. In such a case as the debate about Mytilene in the third book, it is easy to demonstrate that Thucydides knowingly distorted that day's meeting in the Athenian assembly.

He was a genius, and he was a dedicated man. Easy explanations therefore will not do. His difficulties lay very deep; to this day they remain the essential difficulty of all historical writing, and it is the mark of Thucydides' greatness that he appreciated it so early, at the very beginning of historiography. The historian's data are individual events and persons whose sum total is the historical process. Unlike the poet, he must get them right, exactly as they were, and not, in Aristotle's phrase about tragedy, as they might or ought to have been "from probability or necessity". But then what? A mere retelling of individual events in sequence, no matter how accurately captured, would be just that and nothing more. It could be exciting, moving, scandalous, funny, entertaining—but would it be important, would it be worth the pain and effort of a lifetime? Greek intellectuals like Thucydides were in dead earnest about their conviction that man is a rational being. As a corollary, they believed that knowledge for its own sake was meaningless, its mere accumulation a waste of time: knowledge must lead to understanding. In the field of history that meant trying to grasp general ideas about human behaviour, in war and politics, in revolution and government. Thucydides' problem, in short, was to move from the particular to the universal, from the concrete events to the underlying patterns and generalities, from a single revolution (such as the one in Corcyra) to revolution in essence, from a demagogue like Cleon to the nature of demagogues, from specific instances of power politics to power itself.

Undoubtedly, Thucydides did not grasp the complexity of the problem right at the start, nor did he ever find a solution that fully satisfied him. He was constantly probing and experimenting, trying out techniques and refining them. To insure maximum accuracy, he kept his narrative sections rather impersonal, making infrequent comments and allowing the story to unfold by itself. Then, to lay bare what stood behind the narrative, the moral and political issues, the debates and disagreements over policy, the possibilities and the mistakes and the motives, his main device was the speech. Sometimes he chose a single speech out of a number which were made in an assembly or conference, sometimes a pair, which by their diametrical opposition presented the sharpest possible choice of actions. These speeches are in direct discourse, and are very much abridged—a perfectly legitimate procedure. But they are also, without exception, written in the language and style of Thucydides, and that gives the modern reader, at least, some twinges of conscience.

In fact, the speeches in Thucydides raised grave doubts among ancient critics as well. Their effectiveness is beyond doubt: the total impact is overwhelming. The reader is quite carried away; not only does he feel that he has seen the Peloponnesian War from the inside, but he is certain that he knows exactly what the issues were, why things happened as they did. More than that, his understanding seems to come from the actors themselves, not from the historian. To Thucydides' contemporaries, far more than to us, this seemed a natural and intelligible procedure. No people have elevated talk and debate into a way of life as did the ancient Greeks. They talked all the time, in public and in private, and they talked with enthusiasm and persuasiveness. Their literature was filled with talk, from the long speeches and monologues of the *Iliad* and the *Odyssey* to the equally long speeches and debates in Herodotus. And in the very years of the Peloponnesian War there was Socrates, who did nothing *but* talk— a philosopher without parallel, for he never wrote a line in all his long life. But no enlightened reader of Homer or Herodotus believed for one moment that the speeches recorded in their books were anything but the creations of the author, whereas Thucydides gave the impression that he was reporting, not creating.

Even Thucydides' warmest admirers must concede that the speeches, which make up a substantial portion of the work as a whole, are not reporting in the same sense as the narrative. The process of selection has gone too far: the historian has taken responsibility not only for choosing the salient points from actual speeches but also for having the "speakers say what was in my opinion demanded of them by the various occasions". That is what Thucydides often did in the speeches. No one can be certain of his motives in so doing, of course; but given his great integrity and dedication, it seems to me that the only satisfactory explanation for this odd procedure was his desire to penetrate to the final and general truths, his fear that they would not emerge from the details unless he underscored and heightened them in this way. How successful he was is shown by the fact that, to this day, the image of Pericles or Cleon that the world preserves is the one Thucydides created by means of the speeches he had them make.

In a sense Thucydides was too successful. He left no ground for re-examination or alternative judgment. So ruthless was he in stripping away whatever he thought was "romance", or irrelevance, that we simply lack the documentation with which to evaluate Cleon, for example, in any way but Thucydides' own. This man led Athens for several years after the death of Pericles, but Thucydides gives him four appearances only, one of them restricted to a single sentence and one a speech. The picture that emerges is complete and dramatic—but is it right? We do not know. More than that, the picture is intended to represent not only Cleon but the demagogue as a type, the kind of leader who took over when Pericles died and, in the historian's judgment, led Athens to folly and destruction. Having summed up Cleon, Thucydides ignored the others, just as he summed up civil strife in general by one example, that of Corcyra.

No historian has ever surpassed Thucydides in this ability to portray a typical figure or situation, and to do so without seeming to intervene in any significant measure. Pericles' Funeral Oration, the plague, the civil war in Corcyra, the debate between Cleon and Diodotus over what to do with rebellious Mytilene, the account of the oligarchic coup of 411 B.C.—these are what make the book a "possession for all time". The continuous narrative in which they are embedded has another quality and another interest. Without it the big scenes and the main ideas would lose their persuasiveness. It is the painstaking accuracy of the narrative that makes the rest seem so real and convincing. On the other hand, Thucydides was right in his feeling that the mere piling up of details, no matter how carefully chosen and described, would eventually lose its interest. The combination he discovered survives because it is particular and universal at the same time, and because it is in the last analysis a moralist's work.

Thucydides was not an original thinker. The general ideas with which he was obsessed were few and simple. He took a pessimistic view of human nature and therefore of politics. Some individuals and some communities, by their moral qualities, are entitled to positions of leadership and power. But power is dangerous and corrupting, and in the wrong hands it quickly leads to immoral behaviour, and then to civil strife, unjust war and destruction. These are the age-old themes of poets and philosophers. The genius of Thucydides lay in his effort to present them in this new way, by writing contemporary history. In some respects he alone of the ancient historians has a modern (or better, a nineteenth-century) quality: in his concentration on war and politics to the virtual exclusion of everything else, in his research methods, in his concern for the most minute detail. Yet he permitted himself liberties, as I have indicated, which no respectable modern historian would dream of. He did this because he apprehended the limits of history, of the study of specific, concrete events, as well as its possibilities, and he wanted desperately to transcend them. Whether he succeeded without becoming something other than a historian, whether it is possible to succeed in such an endeavour, remains an open question in the study of history.

V

SOCRATES AND ATHENS

"This indictment and affidavit are sworn to by Meletus, the son of Meletus of the deme Pitthos, against Socrates, the son of Sophroniscus of the deme Alopece. Socrates is guilty of not believing in the gods in which the city believes, and of introducing other new divinities. He is also guilty of corrupting the young. The penalty proposed is death."

When Socrates, then seventy years old, was put on trial in his native Athens in 399 B.C., the proceedings began with the clerk of the court reading this indictment aloud to the large (but normal-sized) jury of 501 men, all citizens in good standing over the age of thirty. The Athenian system of government was amateur in the strict sense of the word: there were no district attorneys, scarcely any police, and no professional lawyers. If a crime was committed, major or minor, some individual—acting in a private capacity—had to do something about it. He had to lay a charge before the proper official, as Meletus did, and then he had to attend the trial, mount the rostrum, and present his case to the jury. Meletus was supported by two other men, Anytus and Lycon. When they had taken their allotted time, controlled by a water clock, it was Socrates's turn. He denied the charges, defended his life's work and his ideas, and by direct interrogation challenged Meletus to produce the young men whose religious beliefs he had corrupted.

This took hours, while the jury sat on their wooden benches and the spectators stood about behind them. As soon as the speeches were finished, the verdict was given. Athenian juries, unlike their modern counterparts, had full control of the decision. They were judge and jury together, and there was no appeal from their verdict. Nor did they have an opportunity to discuss the case. They simply filed up one by one and dropped their ballots into an urn. The votes were counted in sight of everyone, and the result was announced immediately: guilty 281, not guilty 220.

When a defendant was convicted in this type of case, the jury had next to fix the penalty, which they did by voting once more, this time on choices put to them by the accuser and the defendant. Meletus asked for the death penalty. In reply, Socrates made a number of counter-proposals; for example, he suggested that as a penalty he be voted one of the highest honours in the gift of the state, namely, maintenance at public expense in the Prytaneum for the rest of his life. Such a proposal was consistent with his refusal to accept any imputation of guilt, but it appeared so frivolous and offensive that, if the ancient evidence is to be trusted, eighty of the jurors now switched their votes, and the majority for capital punishment was a large one, 361 to 140. Socrates then went off to jail and everyone else went home, each juror receiving as pay for the day's work three obols, half a workman's normal wage. A month later Socrates drank the cup of hemlock, having refused his friends' efforts to persuade him to flee the country, and died quickly and painlessly.

This much about the trial of Socrates is clear and straightforward enough. But very little else is, and that is a pity. Socrates and Athenian democracy are both dead, but his trial remains alive as a great myth, and like all myths, it is believed —by those who believe it—to exemplify a universal truth. Here is the proof, it is said, of the tyranny of the majority, of the trampling of the voice of reason and individual conscience by mass rule, of the common man's hatred of the man of genius. Socrates may be dead, but the issues are not. That is why it is still important to know what facts lie behind the myth.

The prime, although not the only, source of the myth is an

early work of Plato's known as the *Apology*. (The Greek word *apologia* means 'defence'; it does not imply that a wrong has been done for which the wrongdoer begs pardon.). This work appeared a few years after the trial and pretends to be the actual text of Socrates's two speeches to the jurors. It is necessary to say at once that it is nothing of the kind. All the proceedings in Greek trials were oral. There were no stenographers, and no official records were kept other than the text of the indictment and the verdict. No one could later report the speeches in full unless the speakers themselves had written them out beforehand and preserved them. This Socrates surely had not done. Instead, the *Apology* is a brilliantly dramatic piece in which Plato's hand is visible in every paragraph. In addition, we have two other accounts of Socrates's trial, both by Xenophon (still others were extant in antiquity but are now lost). These versions do not agree with each other, and in places they are quite contradictory.

Here before our eyes is the mythmaking process at work. These 'apologies' could be written and circulated precisely because there was no authentic text of what Socrates really said. In fact, Plato himself hints elsewhere that, far from making the great speeches of the *Apology*, Socrates gave a bumbling performance. He was no orator but an arguer and conversationalist; what was very effective in small groups of disciples was of no use, and even harmed his case, in a set speech to a large, partly hostile, and inattentive audience. It is doubtful that this mattered much in the actual event: most Athenians had had thirty or forty years to make up their minds about Socrates, and no single speech was likely to have changed anyone's mind in 399 B.C., any more than today. But the death of Socrates mattered very much indeed to his disciples, so much so that they wrote the 'apologies' which, in their view, Socrates *should* have made. That is to say, they took a stand on the issues, on the politics and morals of the

Athenians—which they disliked violently—and on the teaching of Socrates and the meaning of his life. Plato's view of these things was not Xenophon's. Because Plato was by far the greater man and the more persuasive, his view prevails down to our own day. And yet, that is not necessarily proof that he was right.

Paradoxically, it is not what Socrates said which is so important, but what Meletus and Anytus and Lycon said, what they thought, what they were getting at, and what they feared. To begin with, who were they that they should initiate so vital an action? Unfortunately, we do not know anything of consequence about either Meletus or Lycon, but Anytus was a prominent and responsible political figure, with a career of considerable distinction and patriotic service behind him. His participation creates a strong presumption that the prosecution was a carefully thought through step, not a merely frivolous or petty persecution.

And who were the jurors who decided that Socrates must die for what he taught? Every year in Athens there was drawn up a jury panel of 6,000 men, volunteers for the service. For each trial, the requisite number were selected from the panel by lot. Since in 399 B.C. there could not have been more than 20,000 men all told who were eligible to sit on juries, Socrates was tried and condemned by a sizeable percentage of his fellow citizens. We know nothing about them individually, but granting that there may have been a disproportionate number of the very poor, who wanted the three obols; of the very old, who found jury duty an entertaining and exciting way to pass the time (at least that is what the comic playwright Aristophanes alleged in the *Wasps*); and of the richer men, who could afford to give time to their civic duties, the 501 jurors were not a bad sampling of the citizenry. Judging from that sample, the conclusion is that the Athenians were divided about Socrates. More correctly, they were divided on the question of how dangerous he was, for many of those who were willing to acquit thought him either a fool or a bore, or both.

Obviously we cannot know what went on in the minds of individual jurors while they listened to Socrates and his accusers. We cannot say why each man voted as he did. But we do know a lot about their collective experience. The most important fact in their lives was the great war between Athens and Sparta, the Peloponnesian War, which began in 431 B.C. and did not end (though it was interrupted by periods of uneasy peace) until 404, five years before the trial. In 431 Athens was the greatest power in the Greek world, head of a very considerable empire, prosperous, and proud—proud of its position, of its culture, and above all, of its democratic system. "The school of Hellas" it was called by Pericles, and Athenians believed and cherished that claim. By 404 everything was gone: the empire, the glory, and the democracy. In their place stood a Spartan garrison and a brutal, dictatorial junta (which came to be known as the Thirty Tyrants). The psychological blow was incalculable, and there was not a man on the jury in 399 who could have forgotten it.

Nor could they have forgotten the appalling losses of the war. Two great plagues struck the city almost at the beginning, and in the four years 430–426 they carried off about one-third of the population. In 415 Athens made an all-out effort in an invasion of Sicily. That ended in disaster in 413: perhaps half the effective fighting force was killed or missing. Finally, the Thirty Tyrants butchered another 1,500 men, drove many others into exile, and plundered wealthy foreigners for their own personal enrichment.

It is testimony to the vigour of Athenian society that the city recovered as rapidly and completely as it did. The Thirty Tyrants had a short life: they were driven out in 403 by the combined efforts of a handful of the exiles and the survivors at home. The traditional democracy was then re-established, not to be challenged again for nearly a century. One of its first actions was to declare a general amnesty, and so powerful was the spirit of conciliation that both Plato and Aristotle, of all people, praised the democratic leaders for it.

Nevertheless, it is a common view today that Socrates was tried and executed as an act of political vengeance by the restored democracy. It is true that Socrates was no friend of democracy as it was practised in Athens. He criticized it freely and frequently, but on the other hand, he was deeply attached to Athens itself, fought in the hoplite ranks in several battles, and at least once in his life held office. There is nothing here to warrant the political vengeance theory, but there may be among his friends and disciples. One was Critias, the evil genius of the Thirty Tyrants, the most ruthless, brutal and cynical of them all. Critias fell in the fighting that helped bring down the tyranny, and with him died Charmides, another of the Thirty. Charmides was uncle to Plato and well known as a disciple of Socrates. In these two men (and in others), we can understand easily enough how many jurors saw at work a poison which they traced back to the teaching of Socrates. Because of their bitter personal memories of the war and the tyranny, their votes may well have been turned, at least subconsciously, against a man who, they knew (and he himself never denied), had wrong ideas and even wronger disciples.

It is curious, however, that neither Plato nor Xenophon so much as hints at such a motivation behind the trial. How could they have missed this ready-made opportunity to demonstrate the wickedness of democratic rule? In a letter attributed to Plato, not only is the spirit of amnesty praised but, the writer continues, "By some chance, however, some of the men then in power brought my friend Socrates to trial." The writer of the letter—whether that was Plato himself or someone else in the Academy does not matter—was not so incompetent as to have said "by some chance" if he intended "for political reasons", and I suggest that he was fundamentally right, that political revenge will not do as an explanation, beyond its background role in the minds of some jurors. The simple fact is that the indictment accused Socrates of impiety and corruption of the young, and of nothing else. We live in an age which tends to be cynical about such matters: "It's all politics" is the usual comment. Maybe so, but the ancient Greeks took religion seriously on its own terms, and we must, too, if we wish to understand the times.

To appreciate what an Athenian could have meant by 'impiety' (the Greek word is *asebeia*), three things must be kept in mind. One is that Greek religion had become very complicated over the centuries, with a great variety of gods and heroes who had numerous and crisscrossing functions and roles. The second is that their religion had little of what we should call dogma about it, but was largely a matter of ritual and myth. And the third is that it was thoroughly enmeshed with the family and the state. Impiety was, therefore, a very loose notion: a man could be deemed impious for desecrating an altar, for revealing the secrets of a mystery cult, or merely for saying things which were considered blasphemous. But whatever form an act of impiety took, the fundamental point was that it was a public matter: impiety was an offence not only against the gods but also against the community, and therefore punishment was not left to the gods but was taken in hand by the state.

Because of the looseness and vagueness of the concept, its definition rested with the jury in each case. They decided whether or not a particular act, if proved, was punishable under the law. This meant in practice that the frequency of such charges and trials in Athens depended largely on the state of public opinion at any given moment. And the period of the

Peloponnesian War was a bad moment. A decree was passed almost at the outset forbidding, as impious, the study of astronomy, very likely as a reaction to the plague. The first victim, we are told, was the great philosopher-scientist from Asia Minor, Anaxagoras, the friend of Pericles; and there were others. There is further evidence of the upsurge of magic and superstition in Athens in this generation, such as the sudden popularity of the cult of Asclepius, the magical healer; or the appearance of imprecatory tablets (a kind of voodoo magic directed against a personal enemy); or the swarms of private soothsayers, diviners, and oracle-mongers whom Thucydides speaks of with such contempt. In 415 B.C. there was the famous double sacrilege, the profanation of the mysteries at Eleusis and the mutilation of the hermae, which drove Alcibiades into exile (and others to their deaths) and may in consequence have cost Athens the war. We cannot speak with certainty, but I have little doubt that in this affair Alcibiades was framed. A large number of men conspired to perpetrate these acts of impiety. They were followed by months of denunciations and investigations, as a result of which some men were executed and others exiled, and the repercussions were felt in Athens for years.

Against this background, Socrates was accused of a specific form of impiety; namely, that he disbelieved in the city's gods and introduced new ones. In Plato's *Apology* this is denied with great vigour, and there is sufficient and convincing proof that Socrates was in fact a man of very deep piety, and we can safely believe the apologists when they insist that he scrupulously performed the sacrifices and other rites. Besides, it is hard to see why the introduction of new gods should have been an indictable offence when it had been happening right and left just at that time. Not only had Asclepius arrived— he was at least a *Greek* god—but there was also an influx of foreign deities, like the Phrygian Cybele and the Thracian

Bendis, whose shrines were set up with official permission. No one accused Socrates of joining in their worship, but even if he had, there could have been no objection. What was said about him was that he was constantly referring to his inner *daemon*, which talked to him regularly and prevented him from taking wrong courses of action. This was more than the voice of conscience: Socrates plainly believed that it was a *god* who spoke to him. But in a society in which sooth-saying was a recognized profession, that is pretty thin ground for prosecution.

There remains, then, the last and most crucial element in the charge: corruption of the young. Plato's *Apology* stresses (and justifies) Socrates's role as a teacher and allows Socrates to admit that his disciples were the young men with leisure for study—in other words, the sons of the wealthiest citizens. (Some of these young men, it must be remembered, eventually became active partisans of the oligarchic coup in 411 and of the Thirty Tyrants in 404.) In Xenophon's *Apology* there is a dramatic moment when Socrates turns to Meletus in court and challenges him: Name one man whom I corrupted from piety to impiety. Meletus answers: I can name those whom you persuaded to follow your authority rather than their parents'. Yes, replies Socrates, but that was a matter of education, in which one *should* turn to experts and not to kinsmen. To whom does one go when one requires a physician or general? To parents and brothers, or to those most qualified by knowledge?

This interchange, fictitious though it may be, somehow strikes at the heart of the issue. Until some fifty years before the trial, there was no Greek schooling to speak of. Children were taught to read and write and figure by the servants who looked after them, usually old male slaves. Beyond that level, formal instruction was restricted to music and physical training. Men of the generation of Pericles and Sophocles learned everything else by living the life of active citizens: round the dinner table, at the theatre during the great religious festivals, in the Agora, at meetings of the assembly—in short, from parents and elders, precisely as Meletus said they should.

Then, roughly in the middle of the fifth century, there came a revolution in education, especially at Athens. Professional teachers called Sophists appeared. They quickly attracted the young men of means to whom they gave higher education —in rhetoric, philosophy and politics. A very good education it was, too, and at high fees. In the process they developed a startlingly new attitude among their disciples; namely, that morals, traditions, beliefs and myths were not a fixed mass of doctrine to be handed on unchanged and without question from generation to generation, but that they were something to be analyzed and studied rationally and, if necessary, to be modified and rejected. Inevitably, these innovations were looked upon with great distaste and suspicion in many quarters. A kind of know-nothingism developed in reply. In one dialogue, the *Meno*, Plato satirizes this attitude with cold deliberation by making Anytus the spokesman of blind conservatism and traditionalism. "It is not the Sophists who are mad," he has Anytus say, "but rather the young men who pay out their money, and those responsible for them, who let them get into the Sophists' hands, are even worse. Worst of all are the cities who allow them in and do not expel them."

The role assigned to Anytus in this section of the *Meno* is a classic example of Plato's bitter irony. It cannot be taken at face value as a necessarily faithful statement of what Anytus thought and said. But there were many Athenians who did think and say such things. Some of this reaction can be explained in obvious terms: there were then, as there are in all ages, people who dislike anything newfangled, whether in education or politics or woman's dress. But it would be a great mistake to think that this is a sufficient explanation. The age of Pericles and the Peloponnesian War which followed made up a period in which Athenian society—more correctly, a part of it—went through a radical transformation in its outlook, its psychology and its manner of living. The Sophists contributed to this transformation although they did not create it. They symbolized, and made immediately visible, the emergence of a new intellectual class divorced in their thinking from the mass of the citizenry as never before in Athens. Sages like Solon were revered because they expressed in their sayings and their lives the ideals of society as a whole. The new sages did quite the opposite: they tore down the prevailing beliefs and the traditional values, especially in religion and morals.

One may speculate on how this conflict of values might have been resolved had the war not intervened. But the war did intervene. And the plague. Then it was no laughing matter when young aristocrats organized a dining club called the *Kakodaimonistai* (literally, devil-worshippers), whose programme was to mock at superstition. They tempted the gods, for example, by dining on unlucky days; and once, shortly before the Sicilian expedition had been well launched, the citizens of Athens awoke one morning to discover that in the night the sacred hermae which kept guard over streets and house entrances had been mutilated all over the city. There was a limit to how much blasphemy the gods would tolerate: when they had had enough, the whole city would suffer the consequences, not just the individual blasphemers. And so corruption of the young became, in the eyes of many, not a matter of abstract principle but a practical danger to the city at a time when it was already beset with troubles enough.

But what has all this to do with Socrates? Of all the ironic aspects of Plato's Anytus scene in the *Meno*, none is more striking than the way in which Socrates there urges that the

Sophists are the proper teachers of virtue. One of the main, serious themes in many of Plato's dialogues is precisely the opposite, namely, that Socrates was bitterly and totally opposed to the Sophists, to their professionalism and their relativistic ethics in particular. Nevertheless, there was a link in the public mind. The classic exposition is the *Clouds* of Aristophanes, performed at the festival of the Greater Dionysia in March 423. The plot, if I may call it that, is the effort of old Strepsiades, a rich rustic, to cheat his creditors by having his son learn from Socrates the techniques necessary for this purpose. The Sophists, the old man has heard, are experts in making the worse case appear the better, and similar dishonest and immoral arts. In the course of the comedy, the Sophists are depicted as cranks, crackpots and crooks, and the audience hears all the accusations which subsequently emerged, in a very unfunny context, in the trial of Socrates: that the Sophists destroy morals and religion, teaching that the sun is nothing but a golden stone, sneering at the old gods and introducing new ones, and corrupting the young by inculcating disrespect for parents and elders. In one rather long section, Aristophanes drops the buffoonery and burlesque and, in all earnestness and great detail, he praises the good old education of the gymnasium and the palaestra, with its stress on music, athletics and decorous behaviour. In the end, the Thinking Shop burned down, and, as Professor E. R. Dodds rightly remarked, the audience was expected to enjoy the holocaust, and to "care little" if Socrates were burned in it.

It is easy to demonstrate that the picture of Socrates in the *Clouds* is almost totally false. Aristophanes's Socrates is a conglomerate of the scientist-philosophers like Anaxagoras, of the Sophists and of comic invention. Of the real Socrates there is little other than his poverty, and even that is caricatured. I have no idea how much Aristophanes knew, in a systematic way, about the teaching of Anaxagoras and Protagoras and Socrates. But whether he was expert or not, the line he took was that distinctions were irrelevant. The whole lot were corrupters of youth, and what did it matter if one corrupted with his astronomy and another with his ethics, or if one took pay and the other did not? There were several reasons why Socrates was the choice victim for the cruel burlesque of the *Clouds*. He was the best known of the various intellectuals under attack. Most of the others were foreigners who came and went, whereas Socrates was a citizen, a native of Athens, who was always there, in the most public places. He was poor and ascetic, proud of his simple clothes and his bare feet. He was ugly, a serious point. Just imagine small boys gaping from a safe distance at Socrates, with his satyrlike face, talking and talking and talking. Small boys grew up to be members of Aristophanes's audiences, and to be jurors at the trial of Socrates. Aristophanes was surely playing on currently popular themes. Although he did not invent them, he intensified them, and he must bear a heavy responsibility, at a distance, for the eventual trial and execution of Socrates. At least Plato thought so, as is evident from his direct reference to Aristophanes in the *Apology*. And I believe that Plato judged rightly.

The distance from the *Clouds*, however, was twenty-four years. The question still remains: Why was Socrates put on trial in 399? My answer is as unsensational as it could be, precisely the answer given in the letter attributed to Plato: Socrates was indicted by some chance. Anytus and Meletus and Lycon joined together for personal reasons, which we can only guess at. That they were able to do so is no problem: personal grievances have been the root cause of many trials, in Athens as elsewhere. That they *succeeded*, however, can be explained only by the long complicated background I have been describing. It was this chance combination of history and personal factors that produced the great tragedy in 399.

It was not inevitable that Socrates had to be tried and executed. But when he *was* accused in 399, it was immediately probable that the atmosphere which had been building up since 431 would destroy him.

And yet, had only thirty-one jurors voted the other way, Socrates would have been acquitted in spite of everything, so close was the margin. There was no lynch psychology; there are even no indications that public emotions were wildly aroused. No one was creating a martyr. That came afterwards. To the people close to Socrates, and to others who were deeply interested in philosophy, this was no mere personal tragedy but something very much deeper and more universal in its meaning. It was these men who, in the next generation or two, created the symbol and the myth. The actual indictment may have been a matter of chance. But what lay behind it was not; it was inherent in any society in which power lay in the hands of any group simply because it had wealth or numbers or some other purely external qualification. Only the virtuous—the philosophers—should govern; otherwise there could be only evil consequences. Democracy was a particularly sinister form of misrule, but for Plato the death of Socrates symbolized the evil of any open or free society, not just of a democratic one.

It was the nineteenth century, in particular, which abstracted one part from the myth created by Plato and seized on that side of it only, the dangers of mass rule. In truth, the fate of Socrates is a demonstration of the old axiom that eternal vigilance is the price of liberty. Freedom never sits so securely that it may not be harmed by its own upholders. In fifth-century Athens the elements of insecurity were both numerous and strong. There was the chronic poverty of resources, with its never-ending threat of famine; there was the long-drawn-out war with Sparta; there was the fact that freedom and democracy were, by definition, the privilege of a minority and excluded slaves and numerous noncitizens; and there was widespread superstition and irrationalism. There was also a technical weakness in the system. The juries had too much latitude, in the sense that they could not only decide on a man's guilt but could also define the crime he had committed. When impiety—and this is only an example—is a catch basin, no man is safe.

That much can be conceded to the myth in its modern version, but no more. The execution of Socrates is a fact, and it is one of several such facts which reveal that Athenian democracy was not a perfect instrument. It is equally a fact, which both ancient and modern spokesmen for the myth conveniently overlook, that the case of Socrates was isolated in its time. There could be no better witness to this than Plato. It was in Athens that he worked and taught, freely and safely, for most of his long life; and what he taught was hostile, down to its very roots, to much that Athenians believed and cherished. No one threatened him or stopped him. The Athenians are entitled to have their record judged whole for the two centuries in which they lived under a democracy, and not solely by their mistakes. So judged, it is an admirable record, an argument *for* a free society. Ironically both Plato and Xenophon (and some modern historians) idealized Sparta as against Athens. Sparta was the Greek closed society *par excellence*. There Socrates could never have *begun* to teach, or even to think.

VI

PLATO AND
PRACTICAL POLITICS

BERTRAND RUSSELL once wrote that "the value of philosophy . . . is to be sought largely in its uncertainty". Many philosophers would agree, probably most, at least in England: but not all, and until fairly recently, hardly any. Philosophers were long accustomed to look on themselves as the men who were pre-eminently qualified not only to ask the most fundamental questions about human nature and society, about justice and love and morality and piety, but also to find and teach the true answers.

This was certainly the case right through Greek and Roman history after Socrates. To be sure, there were sceptics who were not without influence and there were other philosophers whose ambitions were more modest. But one could go on for hours quoting from ancient philosophers who believed they had discovered *the* Truth. What is far more difficult to determine is the influence, if any, they had outside professional philosophical circles, what practical influence they had on the way individuals behaved and on society more generally; above all, on politics, about which they wrote so much.

What did the ordinary Athenian think about Plato or his work or his school, the Academy? And what are we to think about him, not as a philosopher in the technical sense but about his practical judgments of contemporary politics? One may ask whether, at this distance in time, it is not Plato the philosopher who alone matters, rather than Plato the would-be politician or the opinions of ordinary Athenians. My answer is that all the questions matter. Certain notions about Athens and Athenian democracy which stem directly from Plato have permeated the books most of us were brought up on, books not only about philosophy but also about history and politics and education. I believe these to be false and dangerous notions. I have no intention of debunking Plato; on the contrary, it is precisely because Plato was such a powerful and influential thinker that we must take him seriously and consider his views in their full implications. One has no right to reduce him to just another good chap with some queer ideas, as is all too common among his present-day defenders.

'Defenders' may seem an odd word, as if Plato were in the dock. Yet the fact is that the attack on Plato by Richard Crossman, by Professor Karl Popper in a far more massive way, and by others, has been answered by books with such titles as *In Defence of Plato*. I propose to outflank that controversy and turn to something related but slightly different; I might almost call it 'In Defence of Athens', of Plato's Athens, the Athens he denigrated so successfully. I am not so much concerned with Plato's ideal state or his programme, in other words, as with his picture of Athens as it existed in his day.

Plato was born about 430 B.C. and he died, past the age of eighty, in 347. All his life was spent in Athens apart from an uncertain period after Socrates's death in 399, when he may have removed to Megara and also travelled widely, and there were also his three trips to Sicily. His life thus spanned half that greatest period in Athenian history, from the Persian wars to the year 322, when Athens permanently lost her independence to Alexander the Great's general Antipater— nearly two full centuries of continuous democratic rule, an achievement not to be met in history again until the most modern era. After Athenian democracy was destroyed, for the next 2,000 years—until the American and French revolutions—two vital ideas were effectively eliminated (with brief exceptions) from western society: first, that men are capable of popular self-government; second, that politics are a legitimate and necessary activity in which all members of society ought to take some share and some responsibility. To put it bluntly, if Plato was right about Athens, then we are desperately wrong in our most fundamental political notions today.

1

Before considering Plato and Athens, however, it is necessary to look at the remarkable saga of Plato in Sicily. It was there, we are told, that Plato actually made his one serious effort at practical politics, at translating into practice the ideas about how a state should be run which he worked out in his dialogues, and especially in the *Republic*. At that time eastern and southern Sicily and the southern end of Italy were a populous and prosperous part of the Greek world, having been colonized over a long period beginning about 750 B.C. The biggest, richest, most powerful and most domineering of the Greek communities was Syracuse. In 405, control of Syracuse, which had been a democracy, was seized by Dionysius, then about twenty-five years old (approximately the same age as Plato), who remained in power until his death in 367.

Dionysius became the classic example of a tyrant, both in the Greek sense and in our looser sense of that word. He flinched at nothing—massacre, confiscation, compulsory evacuation of whole cities, large-scale wars with Carthage, piracy—as he built his power in Syracuse, with the aid of mercenaries, into a considerable empire. He was also able to win much popular support in Syracuse and the loyal service of a number of men of education and distinction. Inevitably he became a figure of legend, the tyrant-type for moralists to play with. You can read in Cicero how, like all tyrants,

Dionysius lived in permanent fear of plots and assassination, how, for example, he would allow no one to shave him but his daughters, and how he feared to trust even them with a razor after they had grown up, so that they had then to shave him by singeing his beard with heated nuts.

There is one universal law applicable to all tyrants, absolute monarchs, and despots, enlightened or otherwise, and that is that they need not obey the prevailing rules of their society regarding marriage and the family. Dionysius took two wives in a single ceremony, one from his native Syracuse and the other from Locri in southern Italy. Both wives bore him sons. Dionysius himself wished the succession to fall to his Locrian family, and so, among other things, he named his eldest son in that branch after himself. But when he died a struggle for power was bound to break out sooner or later between the two family groups. The younger Dionysius lacked his father's energy and drive, preferring a soft, luxurious life with perhaps a taste for poetry and a little philosophy. The other faction was led by an enigmatic man named Dion, the forty-year-old brother of the Syracusan wife. Dionysius II gained the upper hand and Dion soon found himself in exile, went to Greece, bided his time there for nearly ten years, and then mounted a military invasion of Syracuse with the support of the Carthaginians. He had a brief temporary success until he was assassinated in the course of a series of ugly double-crosses and murders.

It is hard to imagine a more improbable arena in which to try out Plato's radical political theories, yet that is what the saga would have us believe. It goes like this. Round about 387, Plato made a private visit to the Greeks in the west, where he met the Pythagorean philosophers who thereafter exercised such a profound influence on his thinking, and where he also met Dion, then a youth of about twenty, whom he won over to philosophy and the life of virtue. Twenty

years later, immediately upon the death of the elder Dionysius, Dion invited Plato to Sicily to try to realize the
philosopher-king in the person of the younger Dionysius.
The effort was a fiasco and Dion was forced to go into exile.
Plato nevertheless went back once again, several years later,
this time on the summons of Dionysius II, only to discover
that the latter was not at all serious, to be virtually im-
prisoned for some months, and finally to be allowed to leave.
The aged Plato was at long last disillusioned. The *Republic*
seemed a hopeless Utopia, and so he wrote one more long
work, the *Laws*, in which he laid down in minute and copious
detail the regulations for a second-best kind of state, lacking
philosopher-kings.

There is but one source for this whole story, two long open
letters attributed to Plato, the seventh and eighth in a collection of thirteen. Whenever later writers report anything
about Plato in Sicily, as Plutarch does, for example, in his life
of Dion, they take their information directly or indirectly
from those two letters. Whatever independent information
we possess about Syracuse at this time seems to ignore Plato's
existence. Indeed, such sparse reliable information as we
have about Plato's life altogether comes primarily from the
same two letters. The Greeks of his day had a rare indifference to the private lives of their poets and philosophers. By
the time the gossip-writers appeared on the scene in later
generations, they had little to go on but their imaginations,
out of which poured a fine collection of fictitious and improbable tales.

The two letters have been an embarrassment to some of
Plato's most fervent admirers. Some of the philosophical
ideas expressed ought not to be there: they are consistent
with Plato in his middle years but not with the Plato of the
later dialogues. Worse still, how could Plato have chosen a
tyrant's court for his experiment? He himself had drawn the

bitterest picture of a tyrant in the eighth book of the *Republic*, modelled on the elder Dionysius (whom he does not actually name). Such a tyrant, wrote Plato, comes to power as a demagogue and then finds it to be "his inevitable fate either to be destroyed by his enemies or to seize absolute power and be transformed from a human being into a wolf". True, the younger Dionysius had not seized power; he had been born to it, and the cynic might laughingly suggest that he had not yet been transformed into a wolf and there was hope he could be transformed into a philosopher-king. All other sources are unanimous in their insistence that the young Dionysius was an incorrigible drunkard, Plato alone seeming to be unaware of the fact. Aristotle, for one, says that Dion held Dionysius in contempt precisely because of this grave weakness of his.

As the modern scholarly arguments go on about these difficulties with the two letters, nearly everyone seems to have lost sight of the realities of Sicilian politics. What was actually happening at the moment in Syracuse and what remedies was Plato proposing? Dion's friends, in despair at the turn of events created by Dion's assassination in 354, wrote to Plato for advice. What steps should they take next? In reply they received the long seventh letter, which consists of a few pages of autobiography; some waffle about the great things Dion would have accomplished had he lived, not specified except for the negative point that he would not have permitted a return to democracy; and finally a long disquisition about metaphysics and the theory of knowledge. I doubt if anyone could compose a more useless or empty reply to a request for practical advice. So they wrote again and they received the brief eighth letter, which repeats some of the same ground but finally makes a concrete proposal, namely, that the factions should be reconciled and set up a triumvirate consisting of Dionysius II from one side, and from the other side a son of Dion and a son of Dionysius I by his Syracusan wife, and that there should be a ruling board of thirty-five officials called Guardians of the Laws.

After all his bitter experiences, therefore, all Plato could think of was a sort of collective tyranny within the same tyrant family which had tricked him and mocked him twice over. Nor is the proposal any good even on the lowest level of opportunism. It simply ignores the facts of life in the years 354 and 353. Half Sicily had been dragged into a singularly dirty civil war, in which outright gangsterism had taken over. Each faction, each adventurer, had mercenaries by the thousands, most of them barbarians. Neither lectures on philosophy nor a round-table conference offered much hope. Not once in either letter is there a mention of the mercenaries and the difficulties they would make for any attempt to resolve the civil war peacefully.

Nor is that the end of it. Both letters contain a number of incidental factual statements about the history and constitution of Syracuse. More often than not the writer got his facts wrong—very odd for Plato who in the *Laws* revealed an unparalleled capacity for precision and accuracy in matters of law and constitution. Finally, the letters contain some outright nonsense, of which two examples: On his first visit to Syracuse, the private visit, the letter states that Plato found conditions there unsatisfactory and disagreeable. Because of the tyranny of the elder Dionysius, no doubt? But there is not a word about that. The actual complaint is merely that the people indulged in too much eating and too much sex. Then there is Dion, who, we are told, became a life-long devotee of the life of virtue after that first visit. What did Dion do in the next twenty years, until Plato's return, to demonstrate his spiritual regeneration? The letters do not say. In fact, he became enormously rich in the service of the elder Dionysius, was one of his closest associates, and, I believe, at some point became a Carthaginian agent, which is precisely what the younger Dionysius charged him with when he exiled him.

A possible explanation of these many weaknesses is that the two letters are spurious (as at least two others in the collection surely are). However, the great majority of scholars now hold, against a small but stubborn minority, that they are authentic. I myself have been unable to come to a firm conclusion on this question. In any event, if Plato did not write them himself, then they were written not long after his death by one of his disciples, perhaps by Speusippus, his nephew and successor as head of the school. Whether they emanated from Plato himself or from his immediate circle, the reason they were written and circulated seems fairly clear. Plato and his Academy must have had a bad press for their connection with the whole sordid mess in Sicily, in which several men associated with them in the public mind were implicated. An *apologia* seemed called for; hence the two letters. In the long run they have proved to be an effective *apologia*, whatever their immediate impact, about which we know nothing.

Such an *apologia* raises interesting moral questions; nothing in either letter, however, warrants the view that Plato proposed to convert Dionysius II into a philosopher-king and thus realize on earth the ideal state of his *Republic*. If there is any truth behind the saga, then Plato was surely thinking of the kind of state he envisaged in the *Laws*. But he proved to be wholly incapable of judging, or even of reporting, either the situation or the possibilities realistically. To repeat: none of this bears on Plato the philosopher *as a philosopher*. There have been other great men whose genius deserted them (or blinded them) when they stepped out of their own fields into other subjects, or into the market-place.

2

The seventh letter begins by saying that as a young man in Athens Plato shared the ambition common to his class of taking an active part in public affairs. But, the letter continues, he was soon completely disillusioned: government and laws in Athens were so hopelessly corrupt as to be incurable.

The years of Plato's life were full of extraordinarily interesting and difficult developments in Athens. He was born when the Peloponnesian War had begun, that twenty-seven-year war with Sparta which was such a turning point in Athenian history. The war put an end to the considerable Athenian empire; it cost the Athenians heavily in manpower and public resources; and it twice brought a brief interruption to the democratic regime, once for a few months in 411 and again for about a year at the end of the war in 404, when democracy was displaced by oligarchy, the second time by the brutal rule of the so-called Thirty Tyrants. Athens nevertheless recovered from all the disasters very rapidly, both economically and politically. Throughout the fourth century B.C. she was still a major power in the Greek world, though never again quite the paramount state of the previous century. And in the end she alone was able to mobilize the reluctant Greek opposition to Philip of Macedon and Alexander the Great, in a struggle to preserve independence and popular self-rule. She lost to superior force, but the subsequent history of the Greek world reveals how right that faction was, led by Demosthenes, which insisted that a whole way of life was at stake, and that it was worth fighting for with every possible resource.

And yet much modern writing treats that final century in Athens, from the death of Pericles in 429, with distaste and condemnation. Popular government, we are often told, had become completely irresponsible, the prey of self-seeking and dishonest demagogues; men put their private interests above patriotism; they thought of money-making, not of civic glory and the life of virtue; they were unwilling to fight for their city or even to pay for others to do the fighting. I believe this view to be a caricature, and, rightly or wrongly, Plato is given a considerable share of the responsibility, though not all of it; other writers, such as Aristophanes and Thucydides, bear some too, again rightly or wrongly.

It is true that fourth-century Athens lacked some of the exuberance and excitement of the fifth century, the age of the great playwrights and historians, of the Parthenon, of Pericles. Nevertheless, Athenian morale remained astonishingly high to the very end of the Peloponnesian War, and again later against Philip and Alexander. If the Athenians were slow to appreciate the full threat of Philip, that was largely because they lacked the historian's advantage of hindsight. In the end they showed a far juster appreciation of the issues than many of their modern critics. And it was in the fourth century that Athens really became the "school of Hellas", much more so, in a strict sense, than when Pericles used the phrase in an oration shortly before his death. This corrupt, mob-ruled, vulgar city attracted other Greeks and foreigners by the tens of thousands, and they did not all come for the flesh-pots. Many came to study in the higher schools, now emerging as the best and most famous in all the Greek world, among them Plato's Academy.

The critics of Athens have a trump card, of course—the execution of Socrates in 399. This last of a number of trials for impiety during and right after the Peloponnesian War demonstrates that at the time the people of Athens had retreated in panic from their high ideals. There is no gainsaying that. But are we discussing a perfect society? No one in his right mind claims that for Athens. All governments, of whatever sort, have behaved irresponsibly and viciously at one time or another. Most men, in all societies, tend to look after their private interests first, including their material well-being. To point the finger at Athens on that score, as if that were a vice peculiar to her, is absurd unless one is able to demonstrate that the Athenians were very much more, and more regularly, vicious and self-seeking than other communities. Moreover, 'corrupt' or 'decadent' is not synonymous with 'incurable'. The practical question facing a responsible Athenian at the death of Socrates was whether his community had turned so rotten as to have become incurable; hopeless enough to warrant Plato's total withdrawal from any concern with public affairs. If the trial of Socrates is supposed to be proof that this was the case, it is a singularly weak proof. Not only did legal prosecution for ideas come to an abrupt end, but within a few years Plato himself, not to mention others, established his own school, open to men from all over, where he taught exactly what and how he pleased.

I have said that "rightly or wrongly" Plato is assigned much responsibility for the modern image of a corrupt and decadent Athens, and I put it that way because I believe that he is often appealed to in the wrong way. It is worth noticing that the seventh letter does not lay its main stress on the trial of Socrates as a basis for Plato's disillusionment. A heavier blow had come five years earlier, when the ferociously anti-democratic junta that came to be known as the Thirty Tyrants had been put in charge of Athens by the victorious Spartans. In that group were several relations and close friends of Plato's; he had high hopes in them; and they proceeded to behave very badly. Furthermore, the decision to withdraw entirely from political activity is stated in the letter to be the consequence of a conclusion about the worthlessness not just of Athens or of democracy, but of all other existing forms of government as well.

If we are to conclude from this that Athens had become a hopelessly corrupt society, we must equally conclude that so had every other Greek state. And so is every modern state. They all fail to meet the basic requirements Plato laid down for a just society—some perhaps more than others, but that is a rather minor distinction. What Plato required is not to be found adequately expressed in the brief autobiographical remarks of the seventh letter, a dubious document anyway as I have already suggested, but in several of his dialogues, above all in the two longest, the *Republic* and the *Laws*, the latter written perhaps thirty years later than the former.

The most elemental criticism Plato has is that, whereas the true function of the state is to make men into better men, morally better, both the rulers and the ruled in existing states concern themselves solely with material goods, each man and each faction pursuing special, private interests at the expense of the good of the whole. Since men have false notions of goodness and justice, they pursue false aims, individually and collectively. Behind this criticism lie both an intricate general conception of human nature and a corpus of metaphysical ideas, and the criticism cannot be divorced from them. Plato believed that there are absolute, eternally valid truths, absolute standards of goodness and justice, for example, and that these are knowable. However, since men are unequal by nature—unequal intellectually and *morally*—only a minority are even potentially capable of apprehending the truth, after a long and difficult training programme. The majority can never, under any circumstances, be educated to a point of independent judgment about the basic questions of justice and the like. They must therefore be moulded and ruled by others, in an ideal society by the philosopher-kings of the *Republic*. Such an ideal society, furthermore, being based on absolute and eternal truths, will have no need and no place for change, for opposition, for doubt. Perfection cannot be improved upon; any change would necessarily be for the worse.

In the second-best state of the *Laws*, to be sure, Plato gave up his philosopher-kings and the perfection of the *Republic*. Nevertheless, the later work marked no break on the key question of whether or not the majority of the citizens are to have any freedom of political action, any share in the important decision-making. On that question, the answer was still an unequivocal "No". That is why I cannot agree with the view expressed, for example, by Mr T. J. Saunders in a broadcast on the *Laws*.* "How far away," Mr Saunders said, "the *Republic* seems now." For him, "Plato in action . . . is apt to be much less terrifying than Plato when theorizing". Not for me, however (and the man behind the seventh letter terrifies me even more). I need only quote a few lines from Mr Saunders himself about the state projected in the *Laws*:

> A citizen . . . would quickly find that his freedom to alter the code of law, elect and administer and criticize, was a very limited one . . . there are strict limits to free enquiry and expression of opinion. The state religion is to be powerful and precise in its demands . . . art and literature lay under a strict censorship.

Given all that, it really seems perverse to conclude, as Mr Saunders did, by asserting that Plato's "practical proposals . . . have much in common with the political and social thought of today".

Plato's political philosophy is a coherent, logical construction, worked out with great care and complexity. Few readers of the *Republic* are completely impervious to the power and seductiveness of the arguments (and of the magnificent style). It is superficial and frivolous to parrot from Plato that Athenian democracy was nothing but mob-rule manipulated by demagogues without also accepting both the

* Published in *The Listener*, 22 October 1964.

basis of the criticism and the implications—implications which require the philosopher-king, if not the Big Brother of Orwell's *Nineteen Eighty-Four*. Plato himself never flinched from them. Even in the *Laws* he was still suggesting that the speediest way to introduce a proper constitution was through a young tyrant who was fortunate enough to have the counsel of a true legislator, that is, a philosopher with the right political theory. Hence if there were any truth in the Sicilian story it would not have been inconsistent for Plato to have imagined he might achieve great things by using the younger Dionysius in Syracuse as an instrument, distasteful a step as it may have been, and absurd in practice.

I do not believe that there is a middle ground on the fundamental question. Anyone who holds that the proper function of the state is to bring about the moral perfection of its citizens is playing with very dangerous weapons. If he then anchors his moral judgments in absolute truths, whether they are called Ideal Forms or God, his conviction will lead him, if he is rigorous enough, to believe that he has the right and the duty to impose those absolutes on others for their own good, as in Plato's Republic or the Holy Inquisition or Calvin's Geneva or Orwell's *Nineteen Eighty-Four*. Absolute truths can neither be questioned nor challenged nor flouted. On the other hand, if we do not accept the metaphysical and theological base, or if we share Bertrand Russell's scepticism about final certainty in philosophy, then the whole system built on that base collapses, its programme together with its concrete criticisms of existing institutions. It was a simple matter for Aristotle to expose the poverty and gross inaccuracy of Plato's specific comments on the political and constitutional history of his own time. Viewing affairs as he did from such a vast metaphysical distance, Plato could see no important differences. To him, the earlier Athens of Miltiades or Pericles was already beyond redemption, for—as he wrote in the *Gorgias*, to the embarrassment of his apologists, ancient and modern—even those much-admired statesmen were no better than pastry-cooks, stuffing the gluttonous citizen-body with sweetmeats. As political analysis or historical testimony that kind of remark is simply irrelevant.

It is essential, of course, for the health of a society that there should always be someone to remind us that man does not live by sweetmeats alone. Radical criticism of values and institutions is a function of the political philosopher, as of the political scientist, the sociologist and the historian. But if that criticism is to be of any use as a measuring-rod or touchstone of practical action, and is not to lead to nihilism and abdication of social responsibility, it must at some point come down from the metaphysical stratosphere. It must, as Aristotle said, also "be concerned with the sort of life most men are able to share and the sort of constitution which it is possible for most states to enjoy". For that concern, Aristotle continued, it is no good employing "a standard of excellence above the reach of ordinary men . . . or the standard of a constitution which attains the ideal height".

A close study of Athens can still serve a useful critical function, even after making full allowance for the fact that such a small, relatively self-contained community, with a low level of technology and a simple machinery of government, was able to practise direct democracy, with direct participation by many ordinary citizens in the management of public affairs, in a way that would be impossible today. Such a study, some of us think, turns Plato's criticisms upside down. On the one hand, much of the strength of Athens, in its sense of civic responsibility, for example, came precisely from those things Plato disapproved of most strongly, from the large measure of self-rule and from the extent to which the state helped its citizens satisfy their material requirements as well as their spiritual needs. On the other hand, it was a grave weakness that the citizen body was narrowly exclusive and rested on a very large slave population. On this score the Athenians were too generous for Plato, and he proposed more severe controls over slaves and foreigners.

One of Plato's favourite arguments was to draw an analogy between the state and a ship. Is it logical, he asked time and again, to allow shoemakers and carpenters to make policy in the state, a role for which they have no specialist training? Would you let a carpenter or a shoemaker steer a ship in place of the captain or the steersman? Of course specialists and experts are needed. When I charter a vessel or buy passage on one, I leave it to the captain, the expert, to navigate it—but *I* decide where I want to go, not the captain.

VII

DIOGENES THE CYNIC

WHAT kind of man was Diogenes? He wore a barrel for a cloak and wandered about with a lantern in broad daylight looking for a good man. A favourite of the cartoonists, he has remained for more than two thousand years the most widely known model of the unworldly philosopher, respected and laughed at all in one breath.

Was Diogenes a crackpot, a saint, or a bit of both? It is hard to say, because the legends about him are very ancient and at this distance they cannot be sifted from the facts with any certainty at all. He could have been a teacher of Alexander the Great, as one version has it, but he almost surely was not. He could have been the pupil of Antisthenes, who was a pupil of Socrates, and perhaps he was. He could have been seized by pirates and sold off as a slave, but he probably was not. And so the stories go. In the end, the legends are more important than the reality, for it is the legendary Diogenes who captured the imagination and became the symbol which he has remained throughout history. Debunking legends is a mixed blessing. In this case it would be a great pity, and it is fortunate that we are not able to do so. Otherwise we should have to invent Diogenes all over again, to tell the Alexanders of this world, *Stand out of my way, you are blocking the sun.*

Diogenes was born in the Greek colony of Sinope on the southern shore of the Black Sea, a little before 400 B.C. In his adult years he was forced to leave Sinope because his father was implicated (and perhaps he was too) in some mysterious plot to manipulate or counterfeit the city's coinage. He took up residence on the Greek mainland, alternating between Athens and Corinth, devoted the rest of his life to propagating (and living) the Cynic ideas and the Cynic way of life, and died a very old man, probably in his eighties. Legend puts his death on the same day as Alexander's, which we need not believe. But the times of the two deaths were surely not many years apart, in the same decade in which the greatest of all ancient philosophers died, Alexander's teacher Aristotle.

Athens in the fourth century B.C. was the magnetic centre of Greek intellectual life, and especially of Greek philosophy. And no two men illustrate more completely the variety and contrasts, the richness and the conflicts, than these two foreigners, Diogenes and Aristotle. The latter was a Macedonian from Stagira, son of a physician, fantastically learned, urbane and wealthy, founder of a great school in the Lyceum which rivalled (and even outstripped) the Academy of his own teacher Plato, a prolific writer on nearly every branch of science and philosophy, formal and disciplined in his thinking and writing, systematic, encyclopaedic. Diogenes was in most respects his exact opposite. A wealthy man in Sinope, he lived a beggar's existence now, with a cistern for his home and the streets for his 'school', calculatingly rude and insulting, author of very few works if any (and those in the form of diatribes and mock tragedies), uncompromising in his rejection of all science and learning as useless or worse, a man with a one-track mind and a single interest.

I am looking for a man, was Diogenes's excuse for lighting his lamp in broad daylight. Asked where in Greece he had found good men, he replied, *Men nowhere, but in Sparta boys*. Another time, having returned from Olympia (probably when the games were being held), he was asked whether there had been a great crowd. Yes, he said, *a great crowd but few men*. 'Man' and 'good man' were synonyms in his vocabulary: virtue was the mark of humanity, the one quality which distinguished man from animal. One day he met an athlete who with his friends and admirers was celebrating a great victory and boasting that he was the fastest runner in all Greece. Diogenes's comment was characteristic, and in its way perfect: *But not faster than a rabbit or a deer, and they, the swiftest of the animals, are also the most cowardly.*

That was Diogenes's single track, the search for goodness, for virtue. Nothing else mattered. An unknown Greek poet summed up his existence in these lines: "Without home or city, dead to his fatherland, a beggar, a wanderer, getting his sustenance from day to day." To the poet this was a catalogue of evils; but to Diogenes it was high praise, proof of his remarkable capacity to free himself from externals. When he saw a child drinking out of his hands, he threw away the cup he carried in his knapsack, disgusted with his own weakness: *A child has triumphed over me in plainness of living.*

It is easy to dismiss all this as eccentricity, or worse. And in a way it was. But it was also a radical expression of an unease, a dissatisfaction with Greek society and Greek civilization, with sophistication and material comfort, which had by this time a considerable tradition behind it. The model was, of course, Socrates, and it was not unreasonable though perhaps inaccurate for Diogenes's followers to link him with Socrates by way of Antisthenes. In its earliest phase Greek philosophy had concentrated on great metaphysical speculations about the universe. Then came Socrates and the Sophists, and they, hating each other, together diverted philosophical enquiry from the cosmos to man himself. Ethics, moral behaviour, virtue became the main concern, for Socrates the only really valid study.

Know thyself. That was Socrates's great rule, and Diogenes's too. For both of them it was the hardest of all rules to obey. It meant not self-analysis as a modern Freudian might think of it, but rational insight into man's nature and soul and therefore control and self-discipline: control over the passions, over the animal qualities in man. Furthermore, since man by his nature was a social being, it meant for Socrates an understanding of society, too, of love and friendship and politics, of wealth and civic duty. Ethics was virtuous behaviour in society, not in isolation from other human beings. A Robinson Crusoe could be neither good nor bad, neither virtuous nor vicious (at least not until his man Friday appeared on the scene).

The moral obligation was a twofold one, to live virtuously and to help others to do so. Socrates was therefore a teacher —not in a formal sense, for he had no school and no curriculum, but in the sense that his whole life was devoted to discussion, analysis and guidance, with anyone who would listen, in the places where Athenians normally met and talked, in the barber-shop, in the town centre (the Agora), at dinner-parties. He was also noted for the simplicity of his life, his poverty and bare-footedness and self-discipline with regard to food and drink and sex. But he was no ascetic; he controlled and disciplined the passions, he did not deny them or withdraw from the world of physical appetites and social relationships.

In these respects Socrates was a genuine model for Diogenes. But Plato is said to have called him a Socrates gone mad. The copy had departed too far from the model. Socrates lived plainly, but his rejection of the amenities did not descend to the animal level. Diogenes exaggerated Socratic self-discipline to the point of absurdity, Socratic criticism to nihilism, naturalism to vulgarity and indecency. "It was his habit," writes an ancient biographer, "to do everything in public, the work of Demeter and of Aphrodite alike." *If it is not unnatural to dine*, he reasoned, *then it is not unnatural in the Agora*. Living in a cistern, taking food whenever and wherever he happened to feel hungry, performing bodily functions in the same 'natural' way, defending even cannibalism and incest—all this is part of the legend of Diogenes (and some or all of it may be true).

There is an interesting paradox here: in his search for man Diogenes time and again looked to animals for a model. Animals, too, were natural beings even if inferior, and their behaviour was altogether natural. What was natural was good—that was the great law of the universe, and the wise and virtuous man was he who knew the natural from the un-natural, and who then had the discipline to live according to his knowledge.

This was no new idea of Diogenes's. Nature or human convention (custom)? Which is the correct guide to life? That question had been debated for half a century and more before Diogenes, especially among the Sophists. One had only to look about, and especially to look at Persians and Egyptians as well as Greeks, at Spartans as well as Athenians, to realize instantly that civilized societies had developed a great profusion of rules and regulations, not a few of them flatly contradictory. How was one to judge among them, to sift the good from the bad, the better from the inferior?

Nature and self-sufficiency were the two standards by which Diogenes judged. Not even the Oedipus story could stand up to the test of nature as he applied it. Oedipus's crime was that he married his own mother unwittingly. So what? asked Diogenes. *Domestic fowl do not object to that, nor do dogs or any ass, or the Persians who pass for the elite of Asia.* Here we have the double test of naturalness of which he was so fond, the appeal to animal behaviour on the one hand, and on the other hand the argument that whatever is practised by one group must be natural human behaviour and is therefore proper for all men, their man-made laws (or customs) to the contrary not-withstanding. And here, too, is the perfect example of how far Diogenes was prepared to go, for the Oedipus taboo was as near to untouchability as anything in Greek traditions or beliefs.

There is a child-like simplicity in this kind of reasoning, but then, simplicity is exactly what Diogenes sought. *Happi-*

ness, he said, *consists in but one thing, that a man truly enjoy himself and never be grieved, in whatever place or circumstances he finds himself.* He trained himself to be adaptable, by rolling in the hot sands during the summer or embracing snow-covered statues in the winter. Odd behaviour this may have been, but it should not be confused with monkish self-flagellation and hair shirts, for Diogenes, like Socrates, was no ascetic. "He was not neglectful of his body," writes another ancient philosopher, "as some fools think." He himself said that the wise man *regards the sense-organs given him by nature as gods and uses them rightly . . . , getting pleasure from hearing and seeing, from food and from sex.*

This is the point to self-sufficiency: man is equipped by nature for happiness, but he throws his birthright away and gives himself unnecessary pains and sorrows. *The love of money is the motherland of all evils*, not because it leads man into temptation and foolish and hurtful lusts (Diogenes was no St Paul), but because riches were an unnecessary burden. Like the storks and the cranes, the deer and the rabbits—his familiar animal parallels again—Diogenes shuttled between Athens and Corinth, a distance of fifty miles, to enjoy the mild winters of the one and the cool summer breezes of the other. He insisted that he was thus better off than the king of Persia, who had to travel great distances to achieve the same results. *Besides, my housing arrangements are superior.*

Marriage was like property, a burden and an encumbrance, a hindrance rather than an aid in the satisfaction of natural desires. When asked what was the right time to marry, he replied: *For young men, not yet; for old men, never.* But Diogenes was no celibate in the physical sense. *It is the nature of the gods to need nothing, of god-like men to need little.* 'Need' means 'lack' not 'desire': Greek gods were not celebrated for their chastity, nor was Diogenes.

On these questions, Diogenes may have exaggerated or

contradicted notions frequently discussed and sometimes advocated by other philosophers, from Socrates to Aristotle, but he made no fundamental break with the tradition. Nature and self-sufficiency were familiar concepts, freedom from excessive reliance on externals a familiar virtue. Diogenes's extremism may have been shocking, but it was still permissible. After all, Plato with whom he traded insults unsparingly (at least in the legend) was just as radical when, in the *Republic*, he proposed the abolition of the family and private property for the Philosopher-Guardians.

But then there came the point at which Diogenes pushed too hard and too far. Asked where he came from, he replied, *I am a citizen of the universe*, a phrase which the Greek language expresses in a single word, a *cosmopolitan*. Diogenes coined that word and thereby turned his back on centuries of Greek history. It had been an axiom among the Greeks that their moral superiority rested on citizenship in the free city, whether Athens or Corinth or Thebes or Syracuse. Socrates went to his death rather than leave his city. Plato hated the way Athens was governed and proposed radical reforms, but they were all addressed to the single autonomous city. Even Aristotle, despite the conquests of his pupil Alexander, said that no city could be well governed if its citizens were so numerous that they did not know each other, and its size so great that the herald's voice could not be heard throughout. Diogenes threw all this away, deeming the city but another unnecessary external, like wealth and marriage.

In part, therefore, Diogenes disowned philosophy, for, ever since Socrates, at least, the Greek philosopher had been a critic of society. The arrangements of society were a recognized branch of his subject along with the nature of man. Diogenes's criticism, by contrast, was purely destructive. He merely attacked—politics, social habits and customs, religious practices. Like his hero Heracles he cleaned out the

Augean stables, but he felt no need to put anything new in place of the rubbish. As a cosmopolitan he was bound to no state: a citizen of the universe is a citizen of no place. Therefore he need not find a good form of political organization to replace defective forms.

Nor was that all. Diogenes also disowned most learning, religion and culture. *I marvel that the grammarians investigate the ills of Odysseus when they are ignorant of their own; that the musicians tune their lyre strings while the disposition of their souls is discordant; that the mathematicians gaze at the sun and the moon and ignore matters close at hand.* Like rhetoric and avarice, with which he compares them, they are idle externals, contributing nothing to virtue. Similarly with ritual: to a man performing a purification rite he said, *Unfortunate man, do you not know that lustrations cannot wash away errors, in conduct any more than in grammar?*

In short, Diogenes was a philosopher with very little philosophy, a preacher of virtue who endorsed what most men called vices, a sneerer and destroyer, Socrates gone mad. In the search for man, he brought man very close to the beasts and in his intense concentration on nature, he subordinated ethical interests to bodily needs, much as he would have denied both charges. The wonder, then, is that the Diogenes legend arose in his own lifetime and has remained fresh and strong ever since. Here we are in the realm of hard fact. He was buried near one of the main gates of Corinth and a monument of the finest Parian marble was erected over his grave. It was still standing five hundred years later. Even his native Sinope, which had exiled him, eventually honoured him with a bronze statue inscribed with a verse epigram: Your fame will live on forever Diogenes, for you taught mankind the lesson of self-sufficiency.

The marble monument at Corinth was a dog mounted on a

pillar, for 'cynic' was a common Greek word meaning 'dog-like'. When asked why he was called that Diogenes replied: *I wag my tail to those who give me anything, bark at those who don't, and clamp my teeth in rogues.* Actually the name was originally applied to the Cynics by their enemies, as a sneer, and then adopted by Diogenes and his followers in pride. The sneer was thrown back at the sneerers (much like the word Quaker in more modern times). What the Cynics said in effect was: The grounds on which you call us dogs are just the qualities which make us superior in the one thing which counts, natural self-sufficiency and hence genuine virtue.

There are conflicting explanations given by ancient writers about the origin of the label *Cynic*. But whichever is correct, the important point is that Diogenes drew his following chiefly from the beatniks of fourth-century-B.C. Greece, and it was inevitable that respectable people should have thought them doglike. The Cynic way of life, visible to anyone who cared to look (for they lived and preached in public places, in the open, not in special cafés and clubs), had all the signs of a too literal interpretation of Diogenes's favourite animal analogies. We can only guess what it was that attracted his disciples individually, motives ranging from legitimate and understandable dissatisfaction with the prevailing ideologies and beliefs in some cases, to personal failure, decadence and pure viciousness in others. Parallels are not hard to find throughout history, and in our own time.

What was not inevitable, however, was the long-term success of Cynicism, and its quick rise to perfect respectability. The Stoics, for example, claimed direct ancestry from them: Diogenes's chief disciple, Crates, a wealthy Theban who voluntarily gave up his riches and adopted the Cynic way of life, was the teacher of Zeno, the founder of Stoicism. No effort was made to hide this chain, or to apologize for it. On the contrary, it is in the writings of later Stoics, men like Dio

Chrysostom and Epictetus, that we can still read the longest and most favourable accounts of the philosophy of Diogenes. And Stoicism was in later antiquity the respectable philosophy *par excellence*, didactic, fiercely moral, and in the end the most fashionable of all philosophies. Among the chief Roman Stoics were such men as Seneca and the emperor Marcus Aurelius. Even in the fourth century A.D., Julian the Apostate, the last pagan emperor, a serious intellectual with a strong Stoic streak, was still singing the praises of Diogenes. Less philosophically inclined Roman aristocrats had marble statues of the early Cynic sages in the gardens of their villas, along with their own portraits and statues of the emperors and gods.

There is a paradox here. Later generations of Cynic teachers were not personally converted to respectability. Cynicism became respectable as a doctrine, if one may call it that, while the practising Cynics themselves remained beatniks and cranks, rude preachers and false wonder-workers. A recently discovered document provides an interesting, if harmless, example. In 1950 the University of Geneva acquired in Cairo a group of well over one hundred papyrus fragments, written in a fairly elegant Greek script of the second century A.D., the remains of a manuscript originally in the possession of a man of culture and at least modest wealth. After nearly a decade Professor Victor Martin and his assistants succeeded in assembling the fragments and publishing them, and they turn out to be a collection of Cynic diatribes (the technical, and fully revealing, name for Cynic writings).

The first eight columns contain a legendary dialogue between Alexander the Great and the Indian sage Dandamis, already known from other sources. Then come diatribes in the strict sense, on the superiority of animals over men, for example, which are new, though the ideas are familiar

enough. Finally there is an attack on Homer and other ancient
poets. "I detest them all," writes the anonymous author.
Homer "was a woman-lover. . . . He perpetually insults
Greece because of women and he is admired for his faults.
The *Iliad* and the *Odyssey*, his major works, are about the
adventures of two women, one of whom [Helen] had been
ravished and the other [Penelope] wanted to be. . . . Odysseus
fought at Troy for ten years. Then he spent almost as much
time, in the *Odyssey*, paying court to women, Calypso for seven
years and Circe for a year. Then, becoming satiated, he
longed for Penelope. . . . I do not find that Odysseus the
Wise does anything but dine and chase women."

This is pretty feeble stuff, and by the second century it
was stale stuff, too. Why anyone should have gone to the
expense of having it copied by a good scribe is a question
whose answer lies in the taste of the times. It is also quite
harmless stuff, and that is crucial. Five hundred years earlier
Diogenes and Crates and the other founders of the movement,
despite their nastiness and often cheap humour, were raising
serious questions. The Greek cities, for all their glory, had
failed to maintain peace, either among cities or within the
individual communities. Meanwhile Alexander and his successors were demonstrating that an autocratic monarch, if
ambitious and able, could overthrow the free Greek cities at
will, and could conquer worlds. They opened up new areas
and new possibilities of prosperous material existence, but at
the same time they destroyed the political and personal freedom which lay at the heart of the most advanced Greek cities.

Every thinking Greek was compelled to re-examine his
traditional views and values, and the late fourth century B.C.
was filled with new ideas and challenges to the old. The new
answers varied a great deal, but they had one point in common. No longer was the community the fountainhead of
virtue and the good man linked with the good citizen. Man

now turned inward: virtue and the good life lay in the soul, indifferent to social institutions or political systems. Diogenes was not content with that, however, but insisted on turning the traditional values upside down; he did not preach passive indifference so much as active rejection of the accepted codes of personal behaviour.

The accent falls wholly on the word 'personal'. In no sense was Diogenes a political revolutionary. Beatniks rarely are. Their rejection of social values extends to politics in every form, whether the existing government or system or any other. Therefore, while guardians of public morality may find them a nuisance, they are no danger to society in the direct sense in which even the most insignificant revolutionaries may be considered a threat. On the contrary, they sometimes serve as a convenient safety valve, channelling pent-up resentments and dissatisfactions into possibly unpleasant, but fundamentally harmless, grooves. Men who prefer cisterns to houses, begging to toil, the 'natural' morality of the beasts to the rules of behaviour laid down by the gods, may shock the bourgeoisie, they will never dispossess them.

The legendary stories about Diogenes being put up for sale in the slave market offer a perfect illustration. When the auctioneer asked him what skills he had, according to one version, he replied, *Ruling men*. Then a rich Corinthian approached, Diogenes pointed to him and said, *Sell me to him. He needs a master.*

There is something fine and noble about such stories, with their implication that the good and wise man may triumph over all adversity. But there is equally something weak about them, for they preach acceptance of adversity even when, as in the case of slavery, the condition is made by man and can be changed by man. In the final analysis, the Cynic was a comfortable critic to have hanging about. His attack was too all-embracing to have any effect—he sneered at everything, not only at the things honest men might agree needed reform-ing—and at the same time he called for no action; indeed he decried any action. "Had I not been born Alexander, I should have preferred to be Diogenes." No doubt Alexander the Great never said that. But he could have, quite safely, for he *was* born Alexander.

VIII

ETRUSCHERIA

THE Italians have a word, *etruscheria*, with the same slightly mocking overtone as in *chinoiserie*, and we are apparently in the midst of another floodtide. When even a first-rate professional of many years' experience, Axel Boethius, can close his lively account of 'The Etruscan Centuries of Italy' in *Etruscan Culture, Land and People** with these words,

> . . . never to forget that Etruria was the homeland of renaissance. It was the land which . . . hidden, inscrutable, inner sources of strength has decreed to be the mother earth for the greatest rejuvenation of our western culture since fifth-century Athens

it is obvious that this is a field for the tough-minded alone. With Professor Boethius this sort of thing is no more than an occasional lapse. But when Agnes Carr Vaughan tells us in *Those Mysterious Etruscans†* that "life for the Etruscan was not thought; it was something that was meant to be lived, and lived to the fullest, through the sense and the imagination", we are being asked to take leave of thought ourselves.

The Etruscan 'mystery' has been expounded once for all by D. H. Lawrence.

> Myself, the first time I consciously saw Etruscan things . . . I was instinctively attracted to them. And it seems to be that way. Either there is instant sympathy, or instant contempt and indifference.

Lawrence visited the tombs in 1927, when he was already quite ill. This was a period when life and death and their mystical meaning were often in his mind, and he reacted to

* By Axel Boethius and others, with the collaboration of King Gustav Adolf of Sweden; translated by N. G. Sahlin (New York: Columbia University Press, 1963). Originally published in Swedish in 1960, the book was subsequently reissued in English as a sumptuous jubilee volume for the king's eightieth birthday.   † (New York: Doubleday & Co., 1964).

the Etruscan remains strongly, in a way that was perfectly intelligible in terms of his general philosophy of life:

> The Greeks sought to make an impression, and Gothic still more seeks to impress the mind. The Etruscans, no. The things they did, in their easy centuries, are as natural and as easy as breathing. . . . And that is the true Etruscan quality: ease, naturalness, and an abundance of life, no need to force the mind or the soul in any direction. And death, to the Etruscan . . . was just a natural continuance of the fulness of life.

Unmistakably Laurentian, but is it right or wrong? That is precisely the question one should not ask. As Richard Aldington rightly said in his introduction to *Etruscan Places**, "what Lawrence hoped to give in these sketches was the discoveries of his own poetic intuition, not scholarship." Lawrence was writing about Lawrence all the time. If I want his kind of reaction, I go back to him every time. There is no need to do it again, badly.

To most people, of course, the great 'mystery' of the Etruscans is that of their language. Has it been deciphered? The answer is both no and yes. No one has succeeded in finding a key, as Champollion found the key to Egyptian hieroglyphics or Michael Ventris to the Linear B script of Crete and Mycenae. Yet a large number of Etruscan texts can be read with certainty, and there is no paradox. To begin with, the alphabet of twenty-six letters was borrowed from the Greek and has never been a problem, apart from two or three letters. Of the more than 10,000 texts now known, all but a tiny number are brief, easily apprehended formulas: "I am the jug of Enotenus"; "Memarche Velchana dedicated me" (on a vase dedicated to a deity); "Vel Partuna, son of Velthur and of Ramtha Satlnei, died aged 28." Other words (especially names of gods and titles of officials) were

* (London: Heinemann, Phoenix ed., 1956; New York: The Viking Press, Compass Books ed., 1957).

either taken over from Greek or Latin or entered the Latin vocabulary from Etruscan. By painstaking manipulation of such elements, Etruscologists progress inchwise. Unless further excavation produces a large bilingual text, which is not unthinkable but becomes increasingly improbable with the years, that is the only road to further advance, and the only tempo.

Not everyone has the patience, however, and despite the fact that the history of Etruscan studies is littered with the wreckage of nine-day wonders of decipherment, we have not seen the end of them. Professor Massimo Pallottino, the leading authority on the subject today, rightly complained in *The Etruscans* that the long stream of amateur puzzle-solvers "has brought in its wake the . . . disorientation of all those interested in the Etruscan language", encouraging cynics to "look upon the problem of Etruscan as the favourite playground of cranks or the 'comic' section of linguistic science". Less than a decade after he wrote that, still another claimant has appeared in Dr. Zacharis Mayani, and it is a joyless duty to report of his *The Etruscans Begin to Speak** that there is nothing to his decipherment via Illyrian and modern Albanian, nor, *a fortiori*, in the helter-skelter assortment of ideas and explanations he offers on the basis of his translations.

Fortunately our knowledge of the Etruscans is not restricted to their own writing or there would be little even for the most sensitively attuned romancer to say about them. There are, after all, vast quantities of Etruscan products, ranging from large murals and statues to artifacts down to plain junk (rusted chariot wheels, broken bits of pottery, spearheads, discarded bobby-pins). And there is a considerable body of information, one-sided and uneven in reliability, scattered in Roman writers (and a little among the Greeks too). Mix the ingredients one way and the result is *etruscheria*; combine

* Translated by Patrick Evans (London: Souvenir Press, 1962; New York: Simon and Schuster, 1964).

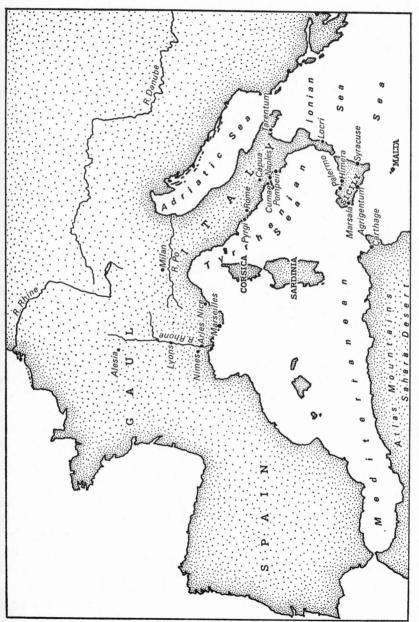

ITALY AND THE WESTERN MEDITERRANEAN

them properly and you end with more questions than answers, but at least they will be the right questions.

The Etruscans themselves believed that they had come to Italy from western Asia Minor (modern Turkey). Greek and Roman writers, from Herodotus on, accepted that tradition, with scarcely an exception. So do modern authorities, also with few exceptions—one of whom, it is only fair to record, is Professor Pallottino. In Italy they found a mixed population, scattered and disunited, unlettered and quite primitive in comparison with the civilizations farther east. By about 700 B.C. much of the region now called Tuscany and Umbria and some parts of Latium had become Etruscan—'become', not just 'ruled by', for the Etruscan language was spoken in all classes of society, and their culture was Etruscan too. From that base, Etruscan influence, colonization and political domination spread north to the Po Valley, south beyond Pompeii. In the course of the sixth century, when the Etruscans attained their apogee, they controlled Rome and it was then that some of the institutions were formed, or transformed, which subsequently helped build Rome into the greatest world power. Yet, so far as the very sparse evidence goes, the Etruscans themselves never united into a single state.

The Etruscans who became the leading force in Italy were not, except for an irrelevant biological component, the Etruscans who came from Asia Minor (if that tradition is correct). As Professor Boethius stresses repeatedly, "If they were immigrants, they merged in town and country with the older population to become an entirely new people." What we call Etruscan culture was a new creation, fashioned in Italy. If one had to hazard a guess as to what the immigrants from Asia Minor contributed which made the new amalgam so dynamic, mine would be in the first instance their ability to exploit the rich metal deposits of the region, and then perhaps a social system better fitted for political expansion, aggression and organization.

At more or less the same time, southern Italy as far north as Naples was being settled by Greeks, beginning about 750 B.C. The Greek sphere marked the southern limit of Etruscan authority, which was overstretched anyway. Rome broke away at the end of the sixth century, the Samnites in Campania half a century later; the Gauls were causing trouble at the Po end; and then the Romans began their steady reversal of roles. Little was left of Etruscan independence by 300 B.C.; nothing, effectively, after 200. Roman conquest also meant gradual Romanization; by 100 B.C. even the Etruscan language was gone except in isolated rural pockets and among antiquarians, while the society in the old Etruscan centres was no longer distinguishable from that of the rest of Italy. Only certain religious practices and notions remained alive, among Romans as much as among people who might still, nostalgically, call themselves Etruscans.

The Greek and Roman literary references we possess to the Etruscans date for the most part after 100 B.C. They look back to a dead past. Although a streak of *etruscheria* seems to have appeared among the Romans then, the prevailing stress was on two aspects, the gluttony, both gastronomic and sexual, of the Etruscans (and especially the licence accorded their women), and the overriding control of religion over their daily lives, including their practice of discovering the will of the gods by examining the livers of animals. Modern writers, almost with unanimity, respond in an odd way: they reject the first aspect as the inevitably false propaganda of the victors defaming the defeated, and they accept the second *in toto*, even exaggerating it until one wonders when an Etruscan, so busy with the performance of compulsory rituals, could have found time to eat, sleep and copulate.

As usual, we turn to Pallottino for a note of sanity: "The

quantitative assessment of religiosity on the part of different peoples runs the risk of losing all reality" without a consideration of the sources of information and the *quality* of the experience. Actually we can approximate a quantitative assessment not of Etruscan religiosity (assuming that is ever possible) but of the attention given to Etruscan religion in the surviving Roman writings, which is not the same thing at all (reminiscent of so much western writing about the Hindus), and which is further distorted by the fact that virtually all Etruscan products come from cemeteries and tombs. This last is inescapable, because the Etruscan urban centres have had a continuous history of settlement to our own day and cannot be properly excavated. It really ought to be unnecessary to explain that if all our information about a society is derived from its cemeteries, the religious side is likely to loom very large. But when Emeline Richardson writes in her *The Etruscans: Their Art and Civilization** that a stone relief from a tomb "shows one of the rare indecent pictures from Etruria", someone must remind her that "indecent pictures" are not habitual in the tombs of any culture, and that she should ask why there were any, rather than congratulate the Etruscans on their restraint.

(The Swedish excavations at San Giovenale, south-west of Viterbo, provide a revealing exception to the endless run of funerary materials. This was a village, the ancient name of which is unknown, that was deserted before the end of the Roman era. The excavators have uncovered a housing complex and fortifications, but not a single inscription nor anything which adds a really new dimension to our knowledge of the Etruscans, valuable though their work has been for the specialist.)

On what grounds do Etruscologists dismiss the persistent image of a much freer code of sexual mores for women than either Greeks or Romans could tolerate? I can find none

* (Chicago: University of Chicago Press, 1964).

other than the unacceptable one implicit in the choice of the phrase, "indecent pictures". No doubt one cannot expect conquerors, least of all the Romans, to be respectful or even honest about a people who gave them so much trouble. It does not follow, however, that everything they said is therefore a lie. There is at least some visible support for the over-eating charge. From the later centuries we have hundreds of reclining, obviously well-fed, fat Etruscan gentlemen in stone on the lids of cinerary urns and sarcophagi. There may be, as Boethius insists, "good reasons for evaluating impartially the peacefully civic life in Etruria's beautiful towns brought into disrepute by the Romans," but we must have the facts right before we evaluate (which, in this instance, means 'judge', a dubious activity anyway). Among the many tens of thousands of Greeks and Romans depicted on pottery, in stone, and in bronze, fat men are very rare and they are always figures of comedy or of contempt. The Etruscans were unlikely to have chosen the coffin as the proper locale for poking fun at its occupant.

The better Roman writers, Livy for example, emphasized that the Etruscans had undergone considerable degeneration after their great age, and that brings us to a central weakness of current *etruscheria*. "Derivative, often downright bad, Etruscan art was always triumphantly Etruscan and never simply uninspired imitation." That sentence from the opening page of Mrs Richardson's central and longest section, on art, typifies the false start from which it is impossible to recover. Imitation is never *just* imitation; that is a truism which by itself does not advance understanding. What is the specifically *Etruscan* quality which makes even bad art "Etrus-can", let alone "triumphantly" that? We must get our time-scales right. The period 700–100 B.C. is considerably longer than the history of the Americas since Columbus. Are we to believe that there was something fixed and omnipotent, uniquely 'Etruscan', working unchanged and always revealing itself through all those centuries? No one believes that, of course. But if 'Etruscan' is a quality which is fluid, then we may no longer dismiss out of hand the Roman insistence that there had been change for the worse; nor may we reserve the Etruscan label solely for the better (a judgment which invariably rests on our standards, not theirs). Read, say, 'German' for 'Etruscan' and it becomes painfully apparent how pernicious an approach this is. And that is without adding the further, more difficult, complication of trying to distinguish between purely external differences (such as can be found in equal abundance between the products of one Etruscan centre and another) and something which one can defend as being qualitative, as revealing national character or specifically Etruscan concepts.

When the Etruscans met the Greeks in southern Italy about 700 B.C., there began a cultural invasion of a scale, intensity and duration for which I cannot think of a parallel. The Etruscan capacity to consume Greek pottery and sculpture, and to make their own in imitation, was boundless. It was also alive, responding to new developments among the Greeks, at times almost instantaneously. Great masses of the stuff made in Etruria were effectively "uninspired imitation" and little else. It is perverse to deny a phenomenon which every student is only too familiar with, though it is unnecessary to go all the way with Berenson's brutal "Only through the originality of incompetence can [Etruscan art] be distinguished from the art of the Greeks." It would be equally perverse to deny that there were also departures from the Greek models, and sometimes rejection. Two questions then present themselves urgently. First, why this passionate addiction to the Greeks, which went so far that the Etruscans preferred to illustrate Greek myths rather than their own on painted pottery and in stone reliefs? Second, what meaning are we to assign to the departures, small or large, whenever it is clear that they were not just the result of technical incompetence? These are the questions that must always be answered about cultural borrowings. Diffusion has to have a recipient as well as a donor; there must be a need to be met, a function to be performed. Too much writing about influences concentrates on the easy half, on the question, Whence?

For the other half we are, in my opinion, blocked with respect to the Etruscans. That is the penalty for having to lean so heavily on the tombs and their contents. The Etruscans buried their dead outside the centres of habitation, preferably in high ground into which they could tunnel their tombs. In common with many ancient peoples, they buried treasure with their dead. This is a practice no longer customary, at least in the west, but archaeology has made it so familiar from the past that it does not strike us as terribly odd. Grave furnishings and tomb architecture fall into two clearly defined types, those intended for the deceased and those intended for the survivors, 'prospective' and 'retrospective', to use the terms proposed by Erwin Panofsky in his brilliant book, *Tomb Sculpture*. The two elements or purposes may be mixed, but essentially we live in a world of retrospective funerary monuments, set above ground where they have a message, whatever it may be, for the living. Etruscan tombs, contrariwise, were primarily prospective, for the use of the defunct and closed off to the living, and what they provided for the dead raises in us thoughts and sentiments which are at once very alien and very seductive, touching the depths of the subconscious. Neither the range of subjects nor the tone and style in which the Etruscans depicted and assembled them were accidental or arbitrary. A whole world of belief was reflected and symbolized, a world with its own strong conventions.

Anyone can read meanings into Etruscan paintings and reliefs, and nearly everyone does, but whose meanings are they as soon as the interpreter steps beyond mere cataloguing?

Whose conceptual world, given the alien-ness of Etruscan life and thinking? The lion was long a favourite subject in Etruscan art. Few if any Etruscan artists ever saw a live lion, and that may explain certain crude blunders, such as their adorning lionesses with the full mane of a lion and with the teats of a bitch, mistakes which their Asiatic prototypes never made. But what explains either the persistence of the lion motif or the transformations the Etruscans imposed on their models? As Llewellyn Brown wrote in his splendid book on the subject, "Throughout this period . . . Etruscan artists were working in highly formalized traditions in which the essential features of the subjects portrayed were reduced to conventional formulae or stylizations, often of pattern-like quality." This applies not only to lions but to Apollos and fat men and sarcophagi and hair-dos. Nearly everywhere we turn we are confronted by this wall of formalism and stylization, and we lack the conceptual key with which to begin an explanation.

That is equally true of politics. We know, for example, that in the earliest period there were kings. But what we know about them is strictly external—that they wore a crown, carried a sceptre and so on. For their functions and powers, in Pallottino's words, "all we may do, is put forward certain suppositions based on analogy with what little is known . . . of the Roman monarchy." The starting-point must be Italy, or sometimes the broader Mediterranean complex, not the obsession with the "triumphantly Etruscan", and everything must be considered within its time. There is no place in this subject for eternal verities. Peculiarities will emerge, in what they refused to adopt or adapt as well as in what they took over, sometimes considerably reshaped. Occasionally we can suggest the historical circumstances which may help to explain what happened. But always by analogy and therefore tentatively, until the day when the Etruscans speak to us in their own words—if such a day ever comes.

IX

THE ETRUSCANS AND
EARLY ROME:
NEW DISCOVERIES AND
ANCIENT CONTROVERSIES

ROME produced no Homer. This is another way of saying
that the Romans, unlike the Greeks and many other
peoples, lacked the tradition—transmitted orally by bards for
many centuries—that once upon a time there had been an age
of heroes who performed deeds of valour against foes of equal
calibre. This is the theme of the *Iliad* and the *Odyssey*, as of
the Anglo-Saxon *Beowulf* and the French *Song of Roland*.
Virgil's *Aeneid* is something very different, the work of a
highly sophisticated poet writing with a considerable literary
experience behind him (more like Dante or Milton than like
the usually anonymous heroic poets), and writing specifically
to fill the gap that the Romans, by then thoroughly imbued
with Greek literature and Greek traditions, had become only
too conscious of.

Heroes fight heroes—that is a pretty universal law. Homer's
Trojans are indistinguishable from his Greeks, except that they
are destined to defeat. But if one asks about Rome's greatest
enemies in its formative and later in its conquering years, a
very different picture emerges—as in Livy's *History*, written
in the same political and intellectual atmosphere as the *Aeneid*,
about five hundred years after Rome broke free from the
Etruscans and two hundred years after they defeated the
Carthaginians under Hannibal. Both the Etruscans and the
Carthaginians had effectively disappeared as peoples by Livy's
time. They had become, apart perhaps from a few isolated
pockets, indistinguishable within the composite population

of Italy and North Africa, respectively, wholly Romanized in the former, less so in the latter. Whatever may have survived of their language, their religion or their institutions was woven into the language, religion and institutions of the regions they had once dominated. Thus, there were a few Etruscan words in Latin and a larger proportion of Etruscan rites and practices embedded in the religion of Italy, but only an occasional Roman antiquarian bothered to (or was able to) identify them as Etruscan elements, and then not always with any accuracy. And such literature of their own as may have existed has been sunk with hardly a trace. All we have, in its stead, is the Roman image of their enemies (plus some Greek elaboration)—nasty, brutish, mean, faithless, licentious. Here and there an individual stands out as something of an exception: Hannibal comes to mind, or the fictitious Dido, Virgil's queen of Carthage. But there are no Etruscan Hectors, no Carthaginian Priams.

It was not so very long ago that this victor's account of the vanquished was still accepted without a second thought. Then came a dramatic shift with respect to the Etruscans (but not the Carthaginians). "Antiquarian research, partaking of the quickened energy of the nineteenth century," led to the discovery of the Etruscan burial sites of central Italy, with their unparalleled artistic treasures. The words I have just quoted open George Dennis's *Cities and Cemeteries of Etruria*, the book that contributed more than any other in the English-speaking world to a new, highly romantic image of the Etruscans which ultimately found its climax in the blood mystique of D. H. Lawrence's *Etruscan Places*. Dennis belongs to that almost legendary group of amateur English explorers and archaeologists who, within a few decades, made the western world aware of the buried and forgotten past of three continents. His two volumes appeared in 1848, the fruits of five years of the most careful and systematic study of the sites and of anything there was to be read on the subject in his day. The work became a best seller.

To read George Dennis now is an exciting experience— and a sobering one: admiration for his energy, boldness and intelligence is tempered by a realization that he (and his contemporaries) got the *history* hopelessly wrong. He (and they) could neither work out the chronological sequence of the archaeological evidence nor penetrate the distortions of the ancient traditions as reported by writers five hundred or more years after the event. He was most wrong in his predictions. The "internal history" of the Etruscans, he wrote, "promises, ere long, to be as distinct and palpable as that of Egypt, Greece, or Rome." More than a century has gone by, and that prediction has not been fulfilled. The reason is perfectly simple: as much as our knowledge of the Etruscans has grown and been corrected since Dennis wrote, it still rests almost entirely on material remains, and, worse still, on remains from tombs and cemeteries almost to the exclusion of anything else. One does one's best to interpret the Etruscan passion for Greek ceramics and for lions, or the enigmatic Etruscan 'smile', or the life-sized sculptures of fat gentlemen reclining on the lids of their sarcophagi.

If the interpretation of artistic conventions is to be anything more than the free play of the interpreter's imagination, he must have a key, which can be provided only by contemporary writing. And there lies the whole trouble. Not, as is widely believed, because the Etruscan alphabet (taken from the Greek) remains an unlocked secret, but because all but a handful of the more than ten thousand available texts are brief formulas, and also because no longish bilingual text turned up.

When the break finally came in July 1964, it was a stunning surprise. It was not the hoped-for document in Etruscan and Latin that the excavators found, but three separate overlapping tablets, two in Etruscan and the third in Punic, the Carthaginian dialect of old Phoenician—in sum, not only the first bilingual text (though not a true one, strictly speaking), but also the first Punic text from Etruria and just about the oldest Punic text ever found anywhere. It is too soon to say how much these will add to our knowledge of the Etruscan language, but they throw unexpected light on a vital phase of Etruscan history and also on ancient traditions concerning the founding of Rome.

The place of discovery was a little bathing resort on the Tyrrhenian Sea some thirty miles west by north of Rome, called Santa Severa. On a rock foundation jutting out over the sea stands a masonry wall built by the Romans in the third century B.C., and within the walled rectangle, a mediaeval castle. Nothing that one can see seems to merit any particular attention, but Professor Massimo Pallottino, the outstanding Etruscologist, decided to organize systematic excavation there in 1957 (under the direction of his pupil, Dr. Giovanni Colonna) because of an old, fragmentary, and tantalizing tradition about the place. Dennis already knew that Santa Severa was called in antiquity by the Greek name of Pyrgi. Virgil lists Pyrgi in his catalogue of Etruscan places, and his contemporary, the Greek geographer Strabo, adds that it had been the harbour for the Etruscan town of Agylla and that it has a temple of Eileithyia, built by the 'Pelasgians', which used to be rich.

Strabo's shift of tenses is intentional: the temple was still standing in his day, but it was no longer important. If the god or goddess was in high repute, an ancient temple was often a storehouse of treasure; both states and individuals regularly made valuable dedications, notably tithes of booty captured in a war or raid. But a rich temple of Eileithyia is rather surprising anywhere, and especially in this region.

Eileithyia was an ancient Greek deity, going back to Mycenaean and possibly even to Minoan times, who was particularly
associated with childbirth and sometimes assimilated to
Artemis, the Diana of the Romans.   As for the 'Pelasgians',
that was just the commonest Greek label for the various in-
digenous peoples of the eastern Mediterranean, about whom
they had only the foggiest—and largely inaccurate—notions.
Strabo implies that Eileithyia's wealth at Pyrgi had been
stolen long ago by Dionysius I, tyrant of Syracuse, an incident
about which we have a slightly longer account from the
Sicilian Greek historian Diodorus, who lived a generation or
two before Strabo. According to Diodorus, in the year 384 B.C.
Dionysius was planning yet another war with Carthage
but lacked funds.   On the pretext of wishing to clear the
Tyrrhenian Sea of pirates, he came to Pyrgi and looted it,
then devastated the territory of Agylla and took many captives,
whom he sold as slaves.   All told, that incursion brought him
the vast sum of fifteen hundred talents, more than enough to
hire and equip a large army.

That is about all, but it is enough to include most of the
peoples who made up the history of this area down to and
beyond the time of Dionysius—'Pelasgians' (whoever they
may have been), Greeks, Etruscans, Carthaginians.   Only the
Romans are missing; properly so, since their role as a great
power lay in the future.   For several centuries southern Italy
and Sicily had been the meeting point of peoples coming from
different directions for different purposes, fighting or raiding
at one moment, having peaceful intercourse at another,
trading, intermarrying, exchanging ideas, amalgamating gods.
Agylla was called Cisra by the Etruscans and Caere by the
Romans.   (Today it is Cerveteri.)   It is not known what the
Etruscan name for Pyrgi was, or how and when the harbour
town came to house the rather curious Greek goddess chosen.
There is nothing surprising about the presence of a Greek

goddess as such; the importation of foreign deities and their assimilation with native gods and goddesses was an unending process in antiquity, inevitable in a polytheistic world filled with contending and clashing peoples. Hence Alexander the Great, for example, was able not only to have himself declared the son of Zeus at a shrine in the Libyan desert dedicated to Zeus-Ammon (the second component being the great Egyptian sun-god), but also to have the announcement quickly accepted by many Greeks without serious opposition.

Now what the excavators of Pyrgi have found so far—and most of the site is still untouched—is not one temple but the foundations of two, lying parallel to each other and facing the sea. The ground plans are typically Etruscan, and they date the older and smaller temple at about 500 B.C., the other perhaps twenty or thirty years later. Eight seasons of the most meticulous digging, photographing, testing and restoring have produced a wealth of stuff of special interest because the site is a great rarity in Etruscology—it is not a cemetery. But nothing touches the discovery of 8 July 1964, in a niche between the two temples: the three tablets already mentioned, carefully folded and of pure gold, no more than one-third to one-half a millimetre in thickness, which, when opened, were revealed to have expertly engraved inscriptions in Punic and Etruscan on them. Even the bronze, gold-headed nails with which the tablets were affixed (conceivably to the doors of the older temple) were preserved. However, no dedicatory objects of any kind accompanied the tablets, and so one plausible suggestion has been offered that the older temple was taken down to be replaced by the larger one and the tablets deposited for permanent preservation on that occasion.

This idea must be treated with considerable reserve at present, as must most other inferences. That I am able to write anything at all detailed on the subject so soon after* the

* Written in 1965.

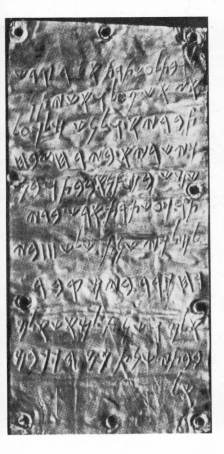
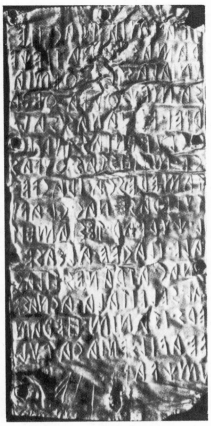

Two of the Pyrgi tablets: the Punic tablet at left, the longer Etruscan one at right.

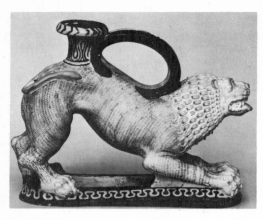

An Etruscan terra-cotta vase (7 inches long), second half of fourth century B.C., found at Vulci.

British Museum

A late Etruscan stone sarcophagus, perhaps mid-second century B.C found in a tomb at Toscanella, now in the British Museum.

Photograph : Mansell Collection

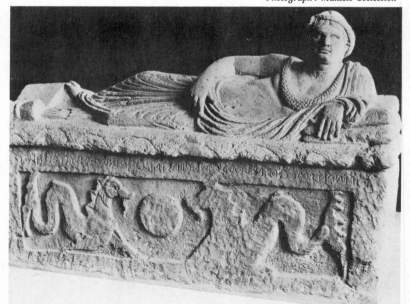

discovery is a tribute to Professor Pallottino, who with his associates proceeded immediately to months of intensive study of the difficult documents. They have translated the Punic text without too many question marks:

> To the lady Astarte. This is the sacred place made and given by Thefarie Velianas, king of Cisra, in the month of the Sacrifice of the Sun in gift within the temple and sanctuary [?] because Astarte has raised [him] with her hand [?], in the third year of his reign, in the month of Krr, on the day of the Burial of the Divinity. And the years of the statue of the goddess in her temple [are as many] as these stars.*

The two Etruscan tablets between them seem to repeat most of the essential information of the Punic one and to elaborate a bit on the cult practices. The writing is in the local style of Caere, which was to be expected, and the dating previously suggested for the two temples on archaeological grounds, about 500–475 B.C., seems to fit the script well enough in a general way.

The overriding question, of course, is why did the ruler of an Etruscan city thirty miles from Rome bow down to the Carthaginian Astarte, the Ishtar of the Bible. Why, furthermore, does the longer of the Etruscan texts call her Astarte-Uni? That combination is of particular interest because Uni was identified with the Roman Juno and sometimes also assimilated to the Greek Hera, consort of Zeus. The three documents, no more than ninety words all together, thus plunge us into the very centre of the political and cultural complex of western Mediterranean history at one of its most critical moments. But they give no further information, not even any clues, which must be sought elsewhere, in the archaeology and among Greek and Roman writers.

* Alternative translations include: "because Astarte commanded [it] through him" instead of "because Astarte has raised [him] with her hand"; and "May the years . . . be as many" in the final sentence.

Archaeology reveals connections between Italy and the eastern Mediterranean well back in the Bronze Age. In particular, southern Italy and Sicily received much pottery from Mycenaean Greece, and especially from the island of Rhodes, in the period 1400–1200 B.C. Then came a rather sudden and long 'dark age', coinciding with a similar dark age in Greece, when the archaeological record is very impoverished and confused for about four hundred years. It was an age initiated by migrations from the north, presumably bringing in for the first time the peoples we call 'Italic'. That is to say, a fairly uniform material culture spread over most of Italy, and the inhabitants spoke closely related dialects belonging to the Italic branch of the Indo-European family of languages. Among them were the Sabines, Oscans, Umbrians, Samnites, Lucanians and Latins. One of the latter, the Romans, ultimately conquered and absorbed all the rest.

At some point in the 'dark age', but one which is impossible to fix, an alien element becomes visible, the Etruscans, whose language is not yet identifiable with any other but is surely not Indo-European. By about 700 B.C. much of the region now called Tuscany and Umbria, and some parts of Latium and Campania, were Etruscan in speech and culture.

Further advance to the south by the Etruscans was blocked by still a third element now in the picture, the Greeks. Beginning about 750 B.C., Greeks began to migrate westward and set up communities along the coast of southern Italy and Sicily, and later in Libya. At about the same time, or perhaps a little earlier, Phoenicians, the most intrepid and experienced sailors of them all, started to establish western trading posts and then genuine settlements in North Africa, on the western rim of Sicily, and on the Spanish coast. In time Carthage became the biggest, richest and most powerful of these, and before 500 B.C. had brought all the western Phoenicians into its sphere.

In a rough way one can plot the groupings on a map: the Italic peoples and the Etruscans in Italy, down to a line running east by south across the peninsula from the Bay of Naples, with the Etruscans also trying to edge their way by sea to Corsica and Sardinia; the Greeks in southern Italy, most of Sicily, and in Libya, also edging into southern France and for a time contending for Corsica and Sardinia; and the Carthaginians in the remaining spaces to the west and also joining in the struggle for the two larger islands. These were not proper national states—the Greeks not at all, and even the Etruscans, who were loosely federated, were never politically unified—and there were no national boundaries. The points of contact were fluid and shifting. (The later and never really justified image of a war to the death between Greeks and Romans on the one hand, and 'barbarian' Etruscans and Carthaginians on the other, must not be read back into this earlier period, nor must the modern notions of racial superiority to which some historians are sadly prone.) It was from Cumae, on the Bay of Naples, for example, that the Greek alphabet, itself a borrowing from the Phoenician, was diffused to the Etruscans and the Latins. It was from the Etruscans that Rome received much of its first political and military organization and its first steps towards urbanization. Greek traders trafficked happily with Etruscans and Carthaginians, and there was a fair amount of settlement of Greeks in Carthaginian towns and vice versa.

This is the kind of relationship reflected in Strabo's brief statement about Pyrgi. No memory had survived that it was the Etruscans who had erected temples there, or of a cult of Astarte, hence the vague attribution to 'Pelasgians'. However, there can be no disputing the considerable Greek influence in Pyrgi both before and after the undoubtedly short-lived introduction of Astarte. That is obvious from the architectural fragments and sculptures now brought to light.

Nor can Strabo have been completely wrong about Eileithyia, though at present we do not know anything more than he tells us on the subject.

Trading often enough shaded off into piracy, and peace was disturbed often enough by short wars. But then, the same was true at the time among the Greek states themselves, in Greece proper and in the west, and among the Italic tribes, even within as closely related a group as the Latins. In the centuries when the Carthaginians and Etruscans were expanding and consolidating their positions almost on an imperial basis— roughly between 700 and 500 B.C.—they tried seriously to agree on spheres of influence, make treaties of friendship, define territories, and guarantee the rights of their traders. Because the Etruscans were not under a single rule, Carthage had to seek these goals by negotiating separately with individual Etruscan cities. The Italians do not seem to have been direct parties to such agreements because they were more backward and because they were accepted by the Carthaginians as fair prey for Etruscan expansion. And the Greeks were in a special position: they alone retained ties with their original homeland and continued to receive recruits for a long time, not always, as we shall see, of a type likely to contribute to peaceful relations with their neighbours.

With this as the background, we can set the Pyrgi documents within a framework of scattered but coherent events reported by various Greek and Roman writers (accepting, for the moment, the ancient statements as all strictly accurate):

540–530 B.C. Greeks from Phocaea in Asia Minor, who had penetrated farther west than any of their fellows (settling at Marseilles and spreading from there along the coast east to Nice and west into Spain), now entered on a phase of organized piracy against both Carthaginians and Etruscans, from a bese on the island of Corsica. The victims joined forces to suppress the Phocaeans, and though the latter won a great naval battle in the waters off Sardinia, it was a Pyrrhic victory. The Phocaeans lost so many men and ships that they had to withdraw, leaving Corsica to the Etruscans and Sardinia to the Carthaginians. Herodotus tells a story that the Etruscans from Agylla (Caere) who were involved in the engagement, then stoned all their prisoners to death, bringing down the wrath of the gods on themselves. They finally sought advice from the Delphic oracle, who told them they could expiate their crime only by instituting regular sacrifices to the spirits of their victims and holding games in their honour. Which, Herodotus continues, they are still doing (that is, in the middle of the fifth century B.C.). And so we have further evidence, in the familiar guise of myth, of a Greek cult in the district of Caere, precisely in the period of the Pyrgi tablets.

524 B.C. The Etruscans, with the support of some of their Italic subjects, attacked Cumae, the oldest Greek settlement in the west and the most powerful Greek community in Campania. They failed, and this marked the end of any serious Etruscan effort to expand southward. It also set off bitter class conflict within Cumae.

509–508 B.C. Rome revolted from Etruscan overlordship, expelled her Etruscan king, Tarquinius Superbus, and set herself up as an independent republic under the Senate and two consuls. (It is characteristic of the tradition that the revolt should be sparked by a personal affront, the rape of the matron Lucretia by the king's youngest son, Sextus, an incident that has become famous in drama and song.) One of the first acts of the new Roman regime was to sign a treaty with Carthage, the effect of which was to define and delimit the movement of Roman traders in Libya, Sardinia and Carthaginian Sicily, and to obtain recognition by Carthage of Rome's political claims in Latium.

494 B.C. After the Persians had suppressed the revolt of the Ionian Greeks in Asia Minor, many Phocaeans fled west under a buccaneering leader named Dionysius and established a base in Sicily from which they resumed the traditional western Phocaean game of piracy against Carthaginian and Etruscan shipping.

480 B.C. The Carthaginians suffered a major military defeat at the hands of Greek forces in Sicily, at the battle of Himera on the northern coast of the island. The background was as follows: The Carthaginians had never made any attempt to settle in, or to control, Sicily, being satisfied with stations located at modern Marsala and Palermo on the sea route from North Africa to Europe. However, in a power struggle among the Sicilian Greeks, the Carthaginians were invited in—and that must be underscored—by the weaker forces as a counterweight, only to be crushed.

In this context the Pyrgi documents become intelligible. The last quarter of the sixth century B.C. marked the turning point in Etruscan history. The defeat at Cumae and the revolt of Rome heralded the slow breakup of Etruscan rule that was to follow, though another three hundred years were to elapse before there were no more independent Etruscan cities left at all. Carthage, which had established a reasonable *modus vivendi* with the Etruscans, could not completely ignore these new developments and allowed itself to be involved, however slightly. Hence the treaty with Rome and the temple of Astarte at Pyrgi. What we cannot know on present evidence is the immediate history behind the activities of the donor, Thefarie Velianas, whose name is inscribed on the tablets (incidentally, Thefarie is the Latin 'Tiberius', one more instance of cultural assimilation). Was he a legitimate ruler —king or chief magistrate—of Caere, or a tyrant who had seized power? The fact that in the Punic tablet he is called *melek*, the ordinary Semitic word for 'king', proves nothing. Was he the first to bring Astarte to Pyrgi, and did he dedicate his golden tablets in the hope of winning Carthaginian support? Or was that the price he was paying for help already given? Help against whom? Whatever the answers, Caere and Pyrgi prospered. They were still rich and under Etruscan rule when Dionysius of Syracuse looted them in 384 B.C. It is anyone's guess as to which deity was in possession of the temple then—mine is that Astarte had long since departed and that the cult was Greco-Etruscan, though perhaps that of Uni-Hera rather than that of Eileithyia.

From the longer historical view, of course, the most important event of the whole complex is the emergence of an independent Rome. The Roman traditions about their own origins and early history did not attain their final form for another five hundred years. No one doubts that the account is filled with improbabilities and outright fictions: it is enough to point out that the city had two different—and equally legendary—founders, Romulus and Aeneas. But how much truth remains at the kernel? That question, long argued by modern historians, has recently become the subject of heated debate again, thanks primarily to Einar Gjerstad, doyen of Swedish classical archaeologists, who is re-examining the archaeology of the city of Rome systematically. He plans a six-volume publication, of which four large tomes have appeared so far under the title *Early Rome*. His main historical conclusions are already known: they have received some support and much criticism, to which the 90 words of the Pyrgi texts have a modest contribution to make.

In bald outline the Roman tradition is that the city was founded in 753 B.C., came under Etruscan rule in 616 (the king being Tarquinius Priscus), freed itself in 509, proceeded to consolidate its position as head of the Latins, and then never looked back. There were few ancient cities without legendary founders, and in this case we need not take either the stories or the date seriously. Archaeology does suggest, however, that the Capitoline and Palatine hills were the first centres of occupation, and this is where the tradition also locates Rome's 'foundation'. From the hills, settlement spread to the old Forum, which they cradled, and to the 'sacred way', running east from the Forum. So far there is no serious argument among modern historians. Trouble begins when the Forum was levelled, given a pebble floor and then a proper pavement, and when 'developed architecture' (as distinct from huts) made its appearance. According to Gjerstad and his supporters, these fundamental new developments fall within the period 575–450 B.C., and he reconstructs the history this way: Rome was not really 'founded' as an urban community until 575, when the earlier separate villages on the hills were united; then came Etruscan rule under kings, and ultimately their expulsion in 450.

Fifty years one way or another does not make much difference, especially when one remembers that archaeological dating must always allow for at least that much margin of error. But this scheme creates more problems than it solves. I shall mention only two of the difficulties. For one thing, it contradicts the one piece of documentation which the later creators of the Roman tradition had to work from—a list, going back to the beginning of the Republic, of the two consuls for each year. Whatever may have been the truth about anything earlier or about occurrences later, that bare list existed, and it seems arbitrary to dismiss all the names of the first half-century as a later invention when there is no good reason why anyone should have wanted to take such liberties merely to shift the establishment of the Republic from 450 to 509.

Second, the proposed new chronology does not fit well into the historical framework of the whole region as I have sketched it. And that is where the Pyrgi tablets help, by shedding new light on Carthage's direct connection with internal develop-

ments in Italy. There have always been historians who disbelieved the treaty of 509 or 508 between Rome and Carthage,
as does the Gjerstad school, on the grounds that Rome was too
insignificant to be allied with so great a power and that it had
no trade of its own worthy of the name, thus making nonsense
of the trading provisions of the treaty. These would be
cogent arguments in isolation. They lose their force when
one remembers that Carthage had been writing just such
treaties with many Etruscan cities. There is, then, nothing
implausible about a renewal of the provisions, repeated more
or less automatically, after Rome broke from Etruscan overlordship. That fits the position about 500 B.C., but not the
international situation half a century later. It fits the date of
the Pyrgi temples and tablets. If a ruler of Caere could be
recognized by Carthage at that time, so could a new regime
in Rome. It would not have been the last time in history that
a new state was permitted to put on airs, at least on paper.

It is necessary to underscore the point that there can be no
defence of the details of the Roman tradition, not even of
what was said to have actually happened in 509. There was
no 'expulsion of the Etruscans' then. There was a political
change which was to have an impact on the future that no
contemporary could conceivably have imagined, but it was
not a change that would leave any traces in the archaeological
record, and especially not in the middle of Rome, a city with
an absolutely continuous history of crowded habitation ever
since. Failure to appreciate that seems to me to be the big
fallacy in the Gjerstad argument.

The border line between a 'legitimate' king and what the
Greeks called a 'tyrant' was a very thin one. Struggles between tyrants and aristocracies were going on all over the
Greek world in the sixth century, and also in Italy, Sicily and
apparently in Carthage. Often the lower classes sided with
the tyrant, as in Cumae after their victory over the Etruscans.

That may have been the situation in Pyrgi, too, and in Rome. The Roman nobles who threw out the tyrant-king Tarquinius Superbus were of mixed Latin-Etruscan (and probably also Sabine) stock. That is why men with unmistakably Etruscan names still appear in the consular lists for the next half-century, until Etruscan names as such were either fully Latinized in Rome, or dropped. The Roman plebs, there is some reason to think, would have preferred rule by Etruscans to rule by their own nobles. Eventually, and for obvious reasons, these aspects of the establishment of the Republic fell from the tradition, to be replaced by a clean-cut patriotic story of noble Romans and brutal, licentious Etruscans.

X

THE SILENT WOMEN OF ROME

THE most famous woman in Roman history was not even a Roman—Cleopatra was queen of Egypt, the last ruler of a Macedonian dynasty that had been established on the Nile three centuries earlier by Ptolemy, one of the generals of Alexander the Great. Otherwise what names come to mind? A few flamboyant, ruthless and vicious women of the imperial family, such as Messalina, great-grandniece of Augustus and wife of her cousin once removed, the emperor Claudius; or the latter's next wife, his niece Agrippina, who was Nero's mother and, contemporary tradition insists, also for a time his mistress. One or two names in love poetry, like the Lesbia of Catullus. And some legendary women from Rome's earliest days, such as Lucretia, who gained immortality by being raped. Even in legend the greatest of them was likewise not a Roman but Dido, queen of Carthage, who loved and failed to hold Aeneas.

Such a short and one-sided list can be very misleading. The Roman world was not the only one in history in which women remained in the background in politics and business, or in which catching the eye and the pen of the scandalmonger was the most likely way to achieve notice and perhaps lasting fame. However, it is not easy to think of another great civilized state without a single really important woman writer or poet, with no truly regal queen, no Deborah, no Joan of Arc, no Florence Nightingale, no patron of the arts. The women of mid-Victorian England were equally rightless, equally victims of a double standard of sexual morality, equally exposed to risk and ruin when they stepped outside the home and the church. Yet the profound difference is obvious.

More correctly, it would be obvious if we could be sure

what we may legitimately believe about women in Rome. Legend apart, they speak to us in five ways: through the erotic and satirical poetry of the late Republic and early Empire, all written by men; through the historians and biographers, all men and most of them unable to resist the salacious and the scandalous; through the letter writers and philosophers, all men; through painting and sculpture, chiefly portrait statues, inscribed tombstones, and religious monuments of all kinds; and through innumerable legal texts. These different voices naturally talk at cross-purposes. (One would hardly expect to find quotations from Ovid's *Art of Love* or the pornographic frescoes from the brothel in Pompeii on funeral monuments.) Each tells its portion of a complicated, ambiguous story. One ought to be able to add the pieces together, but unfortunately there will always be one vital piece missing—what the women would have said had they been allowed to speak for themselves.

> Friend, I have not much to say; stop and read it. This tomb, which is not fair, is for a fair woman. Her parents gave her the name Claudia. She loved her husband in her heart. She bore two sons, one of whom she left on earth, the other beneath it. She was pleasant to talk with, and she walked with grace. She kept the house and worked in wool. That is all. You may go.

Of course it wasn't Claudia who selected and set up this verse epitaph (the translation is Richmond Lattimore's) in the city of Rome in the second century B.C., but her husband or some other kinsman. And it is easy to make cynical remarks not only in this particular instance but in the hundreds of others recording domestic devotion, commonly including the phrase in one variation or another that husband and wife lived together X number of years *sine ulla querella*, "without a single quarrel". Yet there is much to be learned from the very monotony with which such sentiments are repeated century after century, at least about the ideal woman—an ideal formulated and imposed by middle- and upper-class Roman males.

To begin with, until fairly late in Roman history, women lacked individual names in the proper sense. Claudia, Julia, Cornelia, Lucretia, are merely family names with a feminine ending. Sisters had the same name and could be distinguished only by the addition of 'the elder' or 'the younger', 'the first' or 'the second', and so on. In the not uncommon case of marriage between paternal cousins, mother and daughter would have the same name, too. No doubt this was very confusing: a welcome confusion, one is tempted to suggest, since nothing could have been easier to eliminate. No great genius was needed to think up the idea of giving every girl a personal name, as was done with boys. It is as if the Romans wished to suggest very pointedly that women were not, or ought not to be, genuine individuals but only fractions of a family. Anonymous and passive fractions at that, for the virtues which were stressed were decorum, chastity, gracefulness, even temper and childbearing. They loved their husbands, to be sure—though we need not believe everything that husbands said when their wives were dead—but as one loves an overlord who is free to seek his pleasures elsewhere and to put an end to the relationship altogether when and if he so chooses.

'Family' comes from the Latin, but the Romans actually had no word for 'family' in our commonest sense, as in the sentence, 'I am taking my family to the seashore for the summer.' In different contexts *familia* meant all persons under the authority of the head of a household, or all the descendants from a common ancestor, or all one's property, or merely all one's servants—never our intimate family. This does not mean that the latter did not exist in Rome, but that the stress was on a power structure rather than on biology or intimacy. A Roman *paterfamilias* need not even be a father: the term was a legal one and applied to any head of a household. His illegitimate children were often excluded, even when his paternity was openly acknowledged, and at the same time his son and heir could be an outsider whom he had adopted by the correct legal formalities. Theoretically his power—over his wife, over his sons and daughters and his sons' wives and children, over his slaves and his property—was absolute and uncontrolled, ending only with his death or by his voluntary act of 'emancipating' his sons beforehand. As late as the fourth century A.D. an edict of Constantine, the first Christian emperor, still defined that power as the "right of life and death". He was exaggerating, but around a hard core of reality.

Save for relatively minor exceptions, a woman was always in the power of some man—of her *paterfamilias* or of her husband or of a guardian. In early times every marriage involved a formal ceremony in which the bride was surrendered to her husband by the *paterfamilias*: he 'gave her away' in the literal sense. Then, when so-called 'free' marriages became increasingly common—free from the ancient formalities, that is, not free in the sense that the wife or her husband had made a free choice of partner—she remained legally in the power of her *paterfamilias*. Divorce and widowhood and remarriage introduced more complications and required more rules. Where did property rights in dowry and inheritance rest? In the next generation, too, if there were children? The Roman legislators and lawbooks gave much space to these matters. From the state's point of view it was essential to get the power and property relations right, since the *familia* was the basic social unit. But there was more to it than that: marriage meant children, and children were the citizens of the next generation. Not all children by any means, for as Rome extended her empire to the Atlantic and the Middle

East, the bulk of the population within her borders were either slaves or free noncitizens. Obviously the political rights and status of the children were the state's concern and could not be left to uncontrolled private decision. So the state laid down strict rules prohibiting certain kinds of marriage: for example, between a Roman citizen and a non-citizen, regardless of rank or wealth; or between a member of the senatorial class and a citizen who had risen from the class of freedmen (ex-slaves). Within the permitted limits, then, the right to choose and decide rested with the heads of families. They negotiated marriages for their children. And they were allowed to proceed, and to have the marriage consummated, as soon as a girl reached the age of twelve.

The story is told that at a male dinner-party early in the second century B.C., the general Scipio Africanus agreed to marry his daughter Cornelia to his friend Tiberius Gracchus, and that his wife was very angry that he should have done so without having consulted her. The story is probably untrue; at least it is very suspicious because it is repeated about Tiberius's son, the famous agrarian reformer of the same name, and the daughter of Appius Claudius. But true or not, the stories are right in essence, for though the mothers may have been angry, they were powerless, and it is noteworthy that the more 'liberal' and enlightened wing of the senatorial aristocracy was involved. Presumably the wife of the fiercely traditional Cato the Censor would have kept her anger to herself in a similar situation; she would not have expected to be asked anyway. Surely the first of the Roman emperors, Augustus, consulted neither his wife nor any of the interested parties when he ordered members of his family and various close associates to marry and divorce and remarry whenever he thought (as he did frequently) that reasons of state or dynastic considerations would be furthered by a particular arrangement.

Augustus and his family personify most of the complexities, difficulties, and apparent contradictions inherent in the Roman relations between the sexes. He was first married at the age of twenty-three and divorced his wife two years later, after the birth of their daughter Julia, in order to marry Livia three days after she had given birth to a son. At the second ceremony Livia's ex-husband acted as *paterfamilias* and gave her to Augustus. Fifty-one years later, in A.D. 14, Augustus was said to have addressed his last words to Livia: "As long as you live, remember our marriage. Farewell." Livia had had two sons by her previous husband; gossip inevitably suggested that Augustus was actually the father of the second, and the first son, Tiberius, was in 12 B.C. compelled by Augustus to divorce his wife and marry the recently widowed Julia, daughter of Augustus by his first wife. Tiberius was eventually adopted by Augustus and succeeded him to the throne. Long before that, in 2 B.C., Julia was banished by the emperor for sexual depravity, and ten years later the same punishment was meted out to her daughter, also named Julia. That does not end the story, but it should be enough except for two further details: first, one reason for Augustus's getting rid of his first wife was apparently her peculiar unwillingness to put up with one of his mistresses; second, Augustus was the author of a long series of laws designed to strengthen the family and to put a brake on licentiousness and general moral depravity in the upper classes.

Augustus was no Nero. There is no reason to think that he was not a reasonably moral man by contemporary standards (granted that his position as emperor created abnormal conditions). Ancient and modern moralists have a habit of decrying the decline in Roman moral standards from the old days. Talk of 'the good old days' is always suspect, but it may well be that while Rome was still an agricultural community on the Tiber with little power abroad, little luxury, and little

Tombstone of Aulos Kapreilios Timotheos.

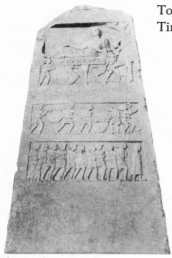

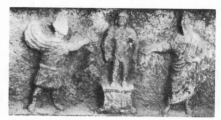

Relief from a tombstone, late first century B.C., now in the Museo Campano, Capua, showing a naked slave on an auction block.

A relief, showing captives, from the marble column of Marcus Aurelius in Rome.

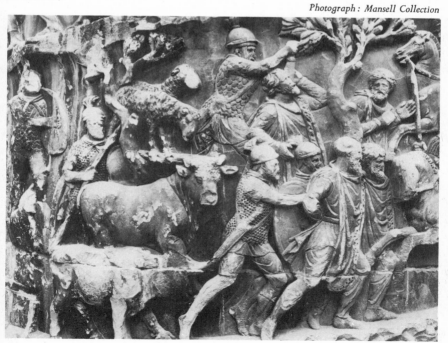

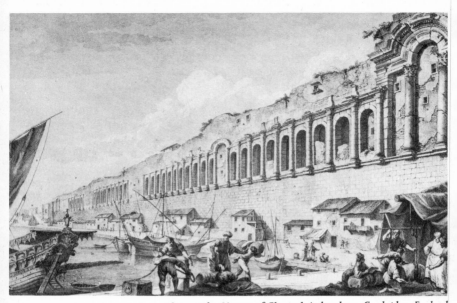

Diocletian's palace at Spalato, drawn by Robert Adam, 1764.

Gold aureus of Diocletian (twice actual size).

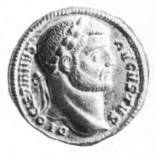

urban development, life was simpler and standards stricter. However, the submissive and passive role of women was very ancient, and certainly by the time Rome emerged as a historic and powerful state, say after the defeat of Hannibal late in the third century B.C., all the elements were already there of the social and moral situation which Augustus both represented and tried in some ways to control. Nor is there any justification for speaking of hypocrisy. No one believed or even pretended to believe that monogamous marriage, which was strictly enforced, was incompatible with polygamous sexual activity by the male half of the population. Augustus was concerned with the social consequences of an apparent unwillingness on the part of the aristocracy to produce legitimate children in sufficient numbers, with the social consequences of extravagant and wasteful living, of *public* licentiousness, and in the upper classes, of *female* licentiousness (which may have been on the increase with the breakdown of political morality in the last century of the Roman Republic). It never entered his mind that moral regeneration might include the abolition of concubines, mistresses and brothels, the end of sleeping with one's female slaves, or a redefinition of adultery to extend it to extramarital intercourse by a married man.

There was no puritanism in the Roman concept of morality. Marriage was a central institution but it had nothing sacramental about it. It was central because the whole structure of property rested on it and because both the indispensable family cult and the institution of citizenship required the orderly, regular succession of legitimate children in one generation after another. There were neither spinsters nor confirmed bachelors in this world. It was assumed that if one reached the right age—and many of course did not, given the enormously high rate of infant mortality—one would marry. Society could not pursue its normal course otherwise. But the stress was always on the rightness of the marriage from a social and economic point of view, and on its legitimacy (and therefore also on the legitimacy of the offspring) from the political and legal point of view. If the relationship turned out also to be pleasant and affectionate, so much the better. It was taken for granted, however, that men would find comradeship and sexual satisfaction from others as well, and often only or chiefly from others. They were expected to behave with good taste in this respect, but no more.

Standards, whether of taste or of law, were profoundly influenced by class. Men like Sulla and Cicero openly enjoyed the company of actors and actresses, but by a law of Augustus and before that by custom, no member of the senatorial class could contract a legal marriage with any woman who was, or ever had been, an actress, whereas other Roman citizens were free to do so. Soldiers in the legions, unlike their officers, were not allowed to marry during their period of service, which was twenty years under Augustus and was raised to twenty-five later on. The reasons for this law were rather complicated, the consequences even more so (until the law was finally repealed in A.D. 197). Soldiers, of course, went on marrying and raising families all the time, and their tombstones are as full of references to loving wives and children as those of any other class. Nor, obviously, could they have acted in this way clandestinely. The law and its agents were not so stupid as not to know what was going on. They merely insisted on the formal unlawfulness of the relationship, and then proceeded to make and constantly to revise regulations for the inevitable confusion : confusion about inheritance, about the status of the children, about the rights of all the parties involved following honourable discharge.

Soldiers apart, we know very little about how these matters worked for the lower classes of Roman society. They were all subject to the same set of laws, but law codes are never automatic guides to the actual behaviour of a society, and neither poets nor historians nor philosophers often concerned themselves in a concrete and reliable way with the poorer peasantry or with the tens of thousands crowded together in the urban rabbit warrens which the Romans called *insulae*. Obviously among these people dowries, property settlements, family alliances for political purposes, and the like did not really enter the picture, either in the establishment of a marriage or in its dissolution. Neither could they so lightly dispense with a wife's labour service, whether on the farm or in a market stall, an inn, or a workshop. It was one thing to "work in wool", as did the Claudia whose epitaph I quoted earlier; it was something quite different to work in wool in earnest.

It would probably be a safe guess that women of the lower classes were therefore more 'emancipated', more equal *de facto* if not in strict law, more widely accepted as persons in their own right than their richer, more bourgeois, or more aristocratic sisters. This is a common enough phenomenon everywhere. No doubt they were freer in all senses—far less inhibited by legal definitions of marriage or legitimacy, less bound by the double standard of sexual morality. For one thing, the rapid development of large-scale slavery after the wars with Hannibal and the Carthaginians, combined with the frequent practice of manumitting slaves, meant that a large proportion of the free population, even of the citizen class, was increasingly drawn from ex-slaves and the children of slaves. This alone—and specifically their experience, as females, while they were slaves—would have been enough to give them, and their men, a somewhat different attitude towards the accepted, traditional, upper-class values. Add economic necessity, slum conditions, the fact that their work was serious and not a pastime, and the rest follows.

In all classes there was one inescapable condition, and that

was the high probability of early death. On a rough calculation, of the population of the Roman Empire which succeeded
in reaching the age of fifteen (that is, which survived the heavy
mortality of infancy and childhood), more than half of the
women were dead before forty, and in some classes and areas,
even before thirty-five. Women were very much worse off
than men in this respect, partly because of the perils of childbirth, partly, in the lower classes, because of the risk of sheer
exhaustion. Thus, in one family tomb in regular use in the
second and third centuries, sixty-eight wives were buried by
their husbands and only forty-one husbands by their wives.
A consequence, intensified by the ease of divorce, was the
frequency of second and third marriages for both sexes,
especially among men. This in turn complicated both personal and family relationships, economically as well as
psychologically, and the prospect, even before the event,
must have introduced a considerable element of tension in
many women. Many, too, must have been sexually frustrated
and unsatisfied.

None of this necessarily implies that women did not passively
accept their position, at least on the surface. It would be a
bad mistake to read our own notions and values into the
picture, or even those of a century or two ago. The women
of French provincial society portrayed by Balzac seem to have
been more suppressed and beaten down than their Roman
counterparts. The latter at least found their men much
more open-handed with money and luxuries, and they shared
in a fairly active dinner-party kind of social life and in the
massive public entertainments. The evidence suggests that
Balzac's women somehow made their peace with the world,
even if often an unhappy and tragic peace, and presumably
so did the women of Rome. We are told by Roman writers
of the educated conversation of women in mixed company.
Ovid in *The Art of Love* urged even his kind of woman not only

to dress and primp properly, to sweeten her breath, to learn to walk gracefully and dance well, but also to cultivate the best Greek and Latin poetry. It is a pity we cannot eavesdrop on some of these conversations, but there is no Roman Balzac or Stendhal, no Jane Austen or Thackeray or Hardy, to give us the opportunity.

This brings us back to the silence of the women of Rome, which in one way speaks loudly, if curiously. Where were the rebels among the women, real or fictitious—the George Sand or Harriet Beecher Stowe, the Hester Prynne or Tess of the D'Urbervilles? How, in other words, did 'respectable' women of breeding, education and leisure find outlets for their repressed energies and talents? The answers seem to lie within a very restricted range of activities. One was religion. It is a commonplace in our own civilization that, at least in Latin countries, women are much more occupied with their religion than are men. But it would be wrong to generalize too quickly: the same has not been true for most of Jewish history nor for most of antiquity. Much depends on the content and orientation of doctrine and ritual. Traditional Roman religion was centred on the household (the hearth and the ancestors) and on the state cults, and the male played the predominant part in both—as *paterfamilias* and as citizen, respectively—notwithstanding that the hearth was protected by a goddess, Vesta, and not by a god. To be sure, the public hearth, with its sacred fire which must never be allowed to go out, was in the charge of six women, the Vestal Virgins. Other rituals were reserved for women, too, such as the cult of *Bona Dea*, the 'good goddess', or such exceptional ones as the formal reception at the harbour, towards the end of the war with Hannibal, of the statue of *Mater Idaea* brought from Asia Minor in response to a Sibylline prophecy which guaranteed victory if that were done. However, the procession was led by a man, "the noblest in the state", as required by the same prophecy. And the Vestal Virgins were subject to the authority of a man, the Pontifex Maximus.

For most of Roman history, then, to the end of the Republic in fact, women were not very prominent even in religion. The change came under the Empire and with the great influx into the Roman world of various eastern mystery cults, carrying their new element of personal communion and salvation. Some of these cults—notably that of Mithras, the soldier's god *par excellence*—were closed to women. Others, however, offered them hope, ultimate release, and immediate status unlike anything they had experienced before—above all, the worship of the Hellenized Egyptian goddess Isis. She became (to men as well as women) Isis of the Myriad Names, Lady of All, Queen of the Inhabited World, Star of the Sea, identifiable with nearly every goddess of the known world. "You gave women equal power with men," says one of her hymns. In another she herself speaks: "I am she whom women call goddess. I ordained that women shall be loved by men; I brought wife and husband together, and invented the marriage-contract."

It was no wonder, therefore, that of all the pagan cults Isis-worship was the most tenacious in its resistance when Christianity ascended to a position first of dominance in the Roman world and then of near monopoly. Christianity itself was soon in some difficulty over the question of women. On the one hand, there was the unmistakably elevated, and for the time untypical, position of women in the life of Christ, and in many of the early Christian communities. Women of all classes were drawn to the new creed. There were women martyrs, too. But on the other hand, there was the view expressed in, for example, I Corinthians 14: "Let your women keep silence in the churches: for it is not permitted unto them to speak; but they are commanded to be under obedience as also saith the law.'' Women were not allowed to forget that Eve was created from Adam's rib, and not the other way round. Neither in this respect nor in any other did the early church seek or bring about a social revolution. Both the ritual of the church and its administration remained firmly in the hands of men, as did the care of souls, and this included the souls of the women.

Where Christianity differed most radically from many (though not all) of the other mystery religions of the time was in its extension of the central idea of purification and purity beyond chastity to celibacy. For many women this attitude offered release through sublimation. That the traditional pagan world failed to understand, or even to believe, this was possible is comprehensible enough. The Roman aristocracy had long been suspicious of the various new cults. A great wave of orgiastic Dionysiac religion had spread in Italy after the wars with Hannibal, soon to be suppressed by the Senate in 186 B.C. Even Isis-worship had a long struggle with the state before achieving official recognition. Anyone who reads the hymns or the detailed accounts of the cult in Apuleius or Plutarch may well find that hard to understand, but the fact is that Isis, though she attracted all classes, was particularly popular in the *demi-monde*.

Sublimation through religion was not the only outlet for pent-up female energies and female rebelliousness. There was another in quite the opposite direction. In the amphitheatres, among the spectators, the women achieved equality with their men: they relished the horrible brutality of the gladiatorial shows (and of the martyrdoms) with the same fierce joy. Gladiators became the pin-ups for Roman women, especially in the upper classes. And at the very top, the women became, metaphorically, gladiators themselves. The women of the Roman emperors were not all monsters, but enough of them throughout the first century of our era, and again from the latter part of the second century on, revealed a ferocity and sadism in the backstairs struggles for power that were not often surpassed—though they were perhaps matched in the contemporary court of the Idumaean dynasty founded by Herod the Great in Judaea. They were not struggling for the throne for themselves—that was unthinkable—but for their sons, brothers and lovers. Their energy and, in a curious sense, their ability are beyond argument. The outlets they found and the goals they sought are, equally, beyond all human dignity, decency, or compassion.

Obviously Roman women are not to be judged by their worst representatives. On the other hand, there must be something significant, even though twisted, in that small group of ferocious and licentious royal females. Under the prevailing value-system, women were expected to be content with vicarious satisfactions. It was their role to be happy in the happiness and success of their men, and of the state for which they bore and nurtured the next generation of men. "She loved her husband . . . . She bore two sons . . . . She kept the house and worked in wool." That was the highest praise, not only in Rome but in much of human history. What went on behind the accepted façade, what Claudia thought or said to herself, we can never know. But when the silence breaks, the sounds which come forth— in the royal family at least—are not very pretty. Most of the Claudias no doubt fully accepted and even defended the values fixed by their men; they knew no other world. The revealing point is that the occasional rebellion took the forms it did.

XI

THE EMPEROR DIOCLETIAN

DRAWING lessons from the past is an old game, to which few rulers have been more subject than Diocletian, Roman emperor from A.D. 284 to 305. He did three things which made this inevitable: he reorganized the administration into an elaborate bureaucracy; he tried to fix maximum prices and wages; and he initiated the so-called 'Great Persecution' of the Christians. Individually and collectively, these measures are a standing invitation to pass moralizing judgments. In his own day there was Lactantius, a convert to Christianity, who in a sadistic pamphlet called *On the Deaths of the Persecutors*, drew the lesson of God's inexorable vengeance. In our day, in the nineteen-twenties, the great Russian-born historian, Michael Rostovtzeff, used Diocletian as a club with which to beat the Russian revolution. Still more recently, journalists and historians have pounced on the welfare state and the American New Deal from the springboard of Diocletian's failure with his edict of maximum prices and wages.

The trouble with so much of this kind of political argument by distant historical analogy is that it too often gets history wrong, or it analyzes actions out of their contexts. If we put Diocletian's career in proper perspective, I shall argue, the supposed modern similarities turn out to be illusory and the modern analogies worthless.

Gaius Aurelius Valerius Diocletianus was a humble Dalmatian who made his career in the army, and on 20 November 284 was proclaimed emperor by a group of officers. We do not know when Diocletian was born, or where, nor do we know much about his rise from the ranks to the throne. All this is fairly characteristic of the period. For half a century the empire had been in complete chaos, and it was pulled together primarily by men from the Danubian regions, mostly obscure men who made their mark and got their power in the army. Those who became emperors soon enough had their biographies written, but biographers of the later Roman Empire were men of little skill and less honour, and what they tell us is irresponsible adulation or vilification, as the case may be, with little fact scattered among the fables.

The years of Diocletian's reign, however, are fairly well documented, not only by his many edicts and laws but also by buildings, which are an important kind of documentation. Lactantius berated Diocletian for his "insatiable passion for building", but, curiously, in his list of examples Lactantius failed to mention the two outstanding ones, the baths in Rome and the palace in Salonae (modern Spalato or Split) on the Adriatic coast of Dalmatia. The baths were the largest in the empire, so vast that today the nearly thirty acres of floor space hold not only the church of Santa Maria of the Angels (which Michelangelo built in what had been the *tepidarium*, the hot bath), but also the larger part of the National Museum of Antiquities. When Diocletian began their construction in 303 he was an old man, and he wanted an appropriate monument for the coming twentieth anniversary of his accession. Such a monument had to be gigantic, megalomaniac, and it had to be in Rome, the 'eternal city' of the pagans which even the Christians looked to as "that city which still sustains all things", the "capital of the world" (in Lactantius's words). Yet, astonishing as it may seem, the "capital of the world" was no longer the real capital of the empire. Diocletian's visit to Rome in 303 was apparently either the first or the second of his life: for almost twenty years the man who ruled the empire and rescued it from chaos had not set foot in Rome. And when he abdicated, in 305, it was not to Rome that he retired but to his native Dalmatia, there to build a great palace modelled on an army camp, with an area of more than nine acres.

The emperor's 'capital' moved with him and his huge retinue, both civilian and military, constantly and restlessly— usually in the Danubian and eastern regions of the empire. His favoured centre was Nicomedia in Anatolia, the city in which he was first acclaimed emperor. It was possible for him to stay so far in the east because in his early reorganization of the administrative system Diocletian had appointed a co-emperor; not his equal in power or authority, but an emperor nevertheless. This second Augustus, an old Illyrian comrade-in-arms named Maximian, administered the west. He too was mobile; in so far as he had a capital it was not Rome either, but Milan. Then, in 293, Diocletian provided Maximian and himself each with a deputy, called Caesar, to help with the government and the army, and at the same time to prepare for eventual succession to the throne. Each Caesar was compelled to divorce his wife and take another; the daughter of Diocletian was given to his deputy, Galerius, while Maximian's stepdaughter was married to Constantius.

The paradox is that by thus splitting up the imperial administration Diocletian saved the empire. Conspiracies against the emperor were as old as the empire itself, but never before had there been anything like the half-century which preceded Diocletian's accession. Between 235 and 284 there were no fewer than twenty Roman emperors formally sanctioned by the Senate. Another twenty or more claimed the title with the backing of an army, and countless others aspired to the claim. These men fought each other and killed each other off at great speed. Diocletian's accession looked like one more such episode, yet in the end he reigned for two decades, and, more remarkable, he lived on after his retirement for another eight years. To achieve this, he also had to survive heavy external pressure all along the borders. A mere list of the peoples with whom he and his associates were engaged in perpetual, and often major, warfare tells the story —Franks, Alemanni, Goths, Sarmatians, Saracens, Persians, and many more. Frontier defence and frontier wars were chronic problems in Roman history, but now they had reached flood-tide, all the more threatening because of their conjunction with the massive internal disorders. The combination had brought the Roman world into a frightful mess: farms pillaged and abandoned, widespread banditry, plague and great losses in manpower, depreciation of the coinage to virtual worthlessness, breakdown in the administrative machinery and in public morality, and an army which was irresponsible, brutal and uncontrollable.

The secret of Diocletian's survival lay in his simple realism. He accepted the Roman world as it was, he reduced its problems to their simplest possible terms, and he made simple solutions, applied with untiring energy, great attention to detail and total ruthlessness. The army was the key, both for good and for evil: the protector of the empire against external enemies and against revolts within, on the one hand, and on the other hand the nursery of pretenders to the throne. Therefore Diocletian enlarged the army, reorganized it, improved the pay and promotion system, and subordinated everything to its needs. To supply the army's food, clothing, weapons and transport, he vastly extended the system of compulsory contributions in kind, embracing the majority of the population of the empire. Then, to keep that system going, he virtually bound people to their farms and their towns, and he greatly enlarged and articulated the civil bureaucracy which had charge of the innumerable operations in which the state was now directly involved. In its details the total system was very complex, but in its principles nothing could be simpler.

There was no deep theory behind Diocletian's programme,

no ideology other than the very elementary one of demanding that all activity be controlled by and dedicated to the needs of the state, as determined by himself, the autocratic ruler, the *dominus* with unbounded authority. Thus, when he saw that the runaway inflation, which had been in process for many years, continued unchecked by his currency reforms, he tried to stop it by decree. The edict of maximum prices and wages of A.D. 301 is absolutely typical both in its simplicity of conception and in the great care with which the details were attended to. The edict covered everything—from partridges to pocket handkerchiefs, and the penalty announced for violation was death for both the buyer and the seller.

The edict failed to hold prices and apparently it was soon allowed to die quietly. But we have little evidence about its working, precisely because it was not very important. Diocletian had no economic theory of money and price. He simply did not like what was happening in this sphere, and so he intervened, as he did in every other sphere. This intervention was not successful, but the whole problem was peripheral, since the essential needs of the army and the state were largely satisfied by direct procurement of the goods and services rather than by purchase. When the edict failed, therefore, some people were hurt, but the state and the army went right on, and since no theory was at stake, there was no need to make a fundamental re-study.

Another failure was the persecution of the Christians. Here there seems not to have been a political issue, as there had been in earlier persecutions. Christians held public office, they were as loyal (or as indifferent) to the state as any other group, there was no great popular demand to crush them, to make them scapegoats for pestilence and famine; in short, there was no visible social or political reason for Diocletian, almost at the end of his reign, suddenly to try to wipe their religion out. Why did he do so? Lactantius tells us in some detail. One day, he relates, when Diocletian was performing a sacrifice, some of his Christian attendants made the sign of the cross, thereby driving away the demons and spoiling the pagan rites. Diocletian lost his temper, and goaded by Caesar, the half-barbarian Galerius, he issued the first of a series of edicts bringing about the 'Great Persecution'. The rest of Lactantius's story is a complicated one, but it is clear that, in his view, the main villain was Galerius rather than Diocletian, and that the motivation lay in pagan piety, coupled with the fury of an autocrat at being flouted—nothing more subtle or complex than that. I see no reason to doubt this view coming from a source so hostile to the emperor and corroborated by the only other important contemporary witness, Eusebius bishop of Caesarea.

The Christians triumphed over Diocletian and Galerius and they never forgave either emperor: Diocletian is most often remembered for his persecution. But from the viewpoint of imperial history that is out of proportion. Neither to the emperor nor to the empire did this episode loom so large. Diocletian went about the persecution with his usual energy and attention to detail, but with less than his usual ruthlessness. I do not wish to underestimate the suffering of the Christian communities, but I do want to get the picture right in its political aspects, as distinct from the moral issues. Whatever else Diocletian may have been, he was not a squeamish man. Nor was this a gentle age. It is significant, therefore, that the number of authentic martyrs in this persecution was very small. This can only mean that, strongly as the autocrat may have felt about the interference in his traditional pagan rites and about the flouting of his will, he never saw in Christianity any threat to his imperial system or power. Furthermore, the failure of the persecution had no important *political* consequences, not even ideologically. The emperor's absolutism remained unchallenged, including his right to determine by decree and penalty the beliefs of his subjects. What Diocletian failed to do, his Christian successors accomplished in reverse. They soon wiped paganism out, by methods no less intolerant and brutal.

Religious intolerance and persecution are wicked and ugly. There is no need to argue that, but it does not follow that they are necessarily doomed to fail, or even to react on the persecutors, at least not in the practical affairs of this life. In another vein, bureaucracy is without a doubt subject to Parkinson's law. But it does not follow that a bureaucratic administration cannot function or accomplish the goals set for it. Yet these are precisely the false inferences which clutter up so much of the thinking and writing about Diocletian. Modern values and moral judgments are confused with practical judgments. The plain fact about Diocletian's reign, whether we like it or not, is that it was a great success. He saved the Roman Empire, so completely that in the east it lived on, much along the lines he laid down, for more than a thousand years—for Diocletian may properly be called the first Byzantine emperor. How many states in history have had a longer life?

Admitting this, some historians go on to say, with the late Professor Tenney Frank, that "the state which Diocletian saved lived under such conditions that it is questionable whether it was worth saving". I completely agree that Diocletian's world was an appalling one. It was shot through with brutality: again I call Lactantius to witness, not for the opposition but in self-incrimination. I have read nothing more disgusting than his long, detailed and complacent description of Galerius's slow, agonizing death from some loathsome disease. It was a world without freedom, without creativity, and without hope: men looked for salvation in the after-life, not here on earth. It was a world of mass servitude alongside outrageous wealth, of bombast and ignorance and dreadful superstition.

It is a mistake, however, to hold Diocletian responsible, except negatively. He made no revolutionary innovations, he merely accepted Roman society and Roman values as they stood in his time, and he made the most of their possibilities. Brutality had been an essential structural feature of Roman society for hundreds of years. 'Bread and circuses' go back to the Republican period—and 'circuses' is a euphemism. The star performer was not the clown but the gladiator and the uncaged wild beast. The population assembled in the amphitheatres for the pleasure of watching wholesale murder. A political policy of calculated frightfulness also went back centuries: witness the destruction of Carthage and Corinth in 146 B.C., the proscriptions of Sulla, or the 6,000 slaves who were crucified on the length of road from Capua to Rome after the defeat of Spartacus.

Diocletian's passion for megalomaniac buildings, to take a different kind of example, was equally traditional. It was the Pont du Gard and the arena in Nîmes, both built under the early emperors, which inspired Henry James to write: "I discovered in them a certain stupidity, a vague brutality. That element is rarely absent from great Roman work. . . . I suppose a race which could do nothing small is as defective as a race which can do nothing great". Diocletian gave his autocracy new trappings, but he was no more absolute in his power than the philosopher-king Marcus Aurelius, a century earlier. He stripped most of the population of the empire of their freedom to choose their place of residence or their work; but a sizeable percentage of this population never had been free.

In sum, ever since Rome became a great empire she had had within her borders large groups of people for whom it could be said that this empire was not worth saving. One aspect of Roman imperial history is the continual enlargement of the unfree sector. Another is the rapid growth of autocracy, from the large amount already present in Augustus to the Byzantine form visible in Diocletian. A third is the decline and disappearance of the positive elements—most of them cultural and artistic—still present in the early days of the empire, if only for the satisfaction of a small minority.

Nevertheless, it is silly to say that by Diocletian's time the state was not worth saving. Apart from the fact that from his point of view—and from that of the army and the bureaucracy and the senatorial landowners—it obviously was worth the effort, the question to ask is: what alternatives were there? So far as I know, no contemporary had any to suggest, not even wildly utopian ones. The intellectuals, pagan and Christian alike, had only the Kingdom of God to offer, which amounted to complete acceptance of the kingdom of Diocletian in this life. Rebellious peasants and slaves, like the Bagaudae in Gaul, whom Maximian fought vigorously in the days of his co-emperorship, wanted nothing more than a change in personnel: they would have liked to become the landlords, while others became their slaves and serfs. More conclusive still, even as an arm-chair exercise, we are unable to think up any alternatives for them, given the material level of life (and especially the low technological level), given the pressure of the barbarians all along the excessively long frontiers, given the nature of the economy and the social system, given the state of knowledge and belief.

It is these basic conditions of life in Diocletian's age which destroy the possibility of fruitful contemporary analogies along the lines which I mentioned at the beginning. Bureaucracy saved Rome, under the conditions of the late third century. That tells us nothing whatever about what bureaucracy may or may not accomplish today. And so with all the other measures adopted by Diocletian. However, there is one plausible generalization, and that is based on the Roman experience as a whole, not on Diocletian's reign alone, and it must be stated conditionally.

A political organism which requires the permanent, forcible subjection of large groups of its population is likely to end by totally brutalizing and stultifying itself. I am not saying that it will therefore destroy itself physically, only that it may destroy itself morally and culturally, which is not the same thing. The question-mark rests largely (though not solely) with the submerged people. Will they just grumble, and accept their fate, or not? Aldous Huxley once said that "the abject patience of the oppressed is perhaps the most inexplicable, as it is also the most important, fact in all history". In Roman history it was virtually a universal fact.

XII

MANPOWER AND THE
FALL OF ROME

THE second half of the fourth century was not one of the
more creative periods in western history, at least not
outside the Church. One would be hard put to think of a
dozen names which merit our attention, and the man who
interests me here has no name known to us at all. He
addressed a pamphlet to an emperor, probably Valentinian I,
in which he put forward proposals for army reform and a
number of ingenious, though perhaps not very practical,
military inventions. In explaining his motives, which he did
at some length and with much carefully self-protective language, he delivered a detailed and slashing attack on the costs
of the almost perpetual warfare of his time, on the oppressive
taxation and the corrupt and extortionate provincial administration of the empire.

One did not lightly criticize in that way in the fourth century; no wonder our man remained anonymous. There is no
way of knowing whether the emperor ever received the
document, but we need have no hesitation in asserting that
the pamphlet, which was probably written shortly before the
shameful disaster at Adrianople at the hands of the Goths in
378, had not the slightest effect on imperial behaviour or
thinking.

Yet the pamphlet survived somehow in manuscript, under
the title of De rebus bellicis ('On Military Affairs'). It was
first printed in a book, with illustrations of the inventions, in
Basle in 1552 and it was reprinted at least five times in the
next two hundred years.* It was read by humanists and

* Most recently by E. A. Thompson in *A Roman Reformer and Inventor*
(1952).

others, who were fascinated by the machines, and by occasional writers on military history. It could have been read by Gibbon, who is known to have possessed two copies and who went through masses of rare and abstruse Latin and Greek texts in preparation for writing his *Decline and Fall of the Roman Empire*. But Gibbon did not read it so far as I can tell, and that is a fact of some significance. To be sure, by Gibbon's time interest in Anonymous's inventions had disappeared and there were better and fuller sources of information about imperial corruption and extortion. However, Anonymous also threw out strong hints about one factor which has impressed some modern students, and that is what we should call manpower shortage. The saving of manpower was one of his strong and explicit arguments in favour of his schemes, and this aspect of the later Roman Empire needs to be looked at with some care.

At its greatest extent, at the accession of Hadrian in 117, the territory of the Roman Empire embraced something like 2,000,000 square miles. If we deduct some very temporary acquisitions we get a more meaningful total of about 1,600,000 square miles. Such a figure may no longer leave us gasping by comparison, say, with the United States or the Soviet Union, but it was still impressive enough. The empire extended from the Euphrates river in Iraq all the way to the Atlantic, the whole of North Africa, Europe below the Rhine-Danube line (and a bit above), and most of Britain along the way. When the empire was functioning properly, furthermore, it was a unified state in fact and not just in name (unlike the Holy Roman Empire of mediaeval and early modern times). It included a large enough number of people, too, but there the figure bears no modern comparison. Actually we do not know the number, nor did any contemporary, not even the emperor himself or his bureau heads. That need not cause any surprise. Modern habits of counting and recording everybody and everything had not yet become sufficiently widespread or necessary (though they were not unknown). A fair guess would be that at its maximum, in the first two centuries of our era, the total population was something like 60,000,000, and that meant everybody—men, women and children, free men and slaves.

The precise numbers do not matter so much when they reach that level. What matters are trends and distribution. How was the population moving in the course of the history of the empire: up or down, or not at all? And how was the population distributed among the social classes and the necessary (or unnecessary) employments? In particular, what proportion was in the army, which was now a wholly professional body, and was that enough?

In the heyday of the empire, say from Augustus to Marcus Aurelius, the army was a fairly modest one of about 300,000 men. Gibbon noticed that this figure was equalled by Louis XIV, "whose kingdom", as he said, "was confined within a single province of the Roman Empire". But the army was sufficient for its purposes; it kept the peace within the empire; it could cope with rebellions, such as the Jewish revolt of 66–70, though that might require time; it protected the frontiers; it was even able to make a few further conquests, including Britain. Then one day it became inadequate, too small in number and sometimes unreliable in performance. The turning point was the reign of Marcus Aurelius (who died in the year 180). The Germanic tribes in central Europe, which had been fitfully troublesome for several centuries, now began a new and much heavier pressure on the frontiers which never stopped until the western empire finally came to an end as a political organism.

We must be careful here not to make too much use of our hindsight. Yet surely there were few Roman leaders, whether emperors or senators or field commanders, so stupid that they did not realize the enormity of Rome's difficulties and the need for effort on a greater scale than had been required before. They did make efforts, and they failed. It is astonishing that they did not fail earlier. In the third century the armies were busier with civil war and politics than with the frontier menace, as they had been once before after the assassination of Nero. For fifty years emperors and claimants to the throne came and went in an endless succession. Then Diocletian restored order, reorganized the administration and the defences, and doubled the army strength, at least on paper. And still the Germans came and the losing struggle against them went on, while civil wars and general disorganization kept recurring.

There was the open symptom of the coming fall of Rome. And this is how Gibbon saw it:

> The timid and luxurious inhabitants of a declining empire must be allured into the service by the hopes of profit, or compelled by the dread of punishment. . . . Such was the horror for the profession of a soldier, which had affected the minds of the degenerate Romans, that many of the youth . . . chose to cut off the fingers of their right hand to escape from being pressed into service.

Note the language carefully: "timid and luxurious", "declining empire", "degenerate Romans". Even if one were to accept the characterization—and I am not concerned to argue that now—it does not explain. One would still have to give reasons why the Romans had become "timid" and "degenerate", if that is what they now were. Professor A. H. M. Jones does not use language of that kind in his great three-volume work on the later Roman Emperor. That is not simply because he has a different set of values from Gibbon's, but because historians now put different questions to the past, and therefore come out with a different picture. Jones's *Later Roman Empire* covers the same ground as the first half of Gibbon's

Decline and Fall. The chief actors are the same; so are the dates and the battles and the defeats. But the history somehow is not the same in the end; the focus has been changed, as is clear on this question of manpower.

The paper strength of the army after Diocletian was about 600,000, a very small figure by contrast with the armies which a modern state with the same total population can muster in wartime. Why, then, were Diocletian and his successors unable to put even their full paper strength into the field against the barbarians, let alone increase the levies? Certainly the stakes were high, the emergency critical. Patriotism in the Roman Empire may have been lukewarm at best: the ordinary man, regardless of class, felt no personal obligation to fight to defend it. That is true, but it is equally true that they wanted even less to have the empire ripped apart by invading Germans. The Roman Empire, despite all its troubles, its burdensome taxation and terrible poverty, its bitter conflicts between Christians and pagans and then among the orthodox Christians and the heretics, was nevertheless an integral part of the order of things, central and eternal. When a Visigothic army led by its king Alaric captured the city of Rome in the summer of 410, St Jerome, then living in Bethlehem, added these words to the preface of the *Commentaries on Ezekiel* he was writing: ". . . the brightest light of the whole world was extinguished . . . the Roman Empire was deprived of its head . . . , to speak more correctly, the whole world perished in one city. . . ."

One reason for the astonishment was that Roman armies still fought well most of the time. In any straight fight they could, and they usually did, defeat superior numbers of Germans, because they were better trained, better equipped, better led. What they could not do was cope indefinitely with this kind of enemy. They were not warring with a neighbouring state like themselves, but with migratory tribes who wanted to loot or to settle in the richer world of the empire. As early as the reign of Marcus Aurelius groups of Germans were allowed to settle on the land and to join the Roman army themselves. That did not work either, though the attempt was repeated many times, partly because they would not be Romanized but chiefly because it simply encouraged more Germans on the outside to demand the same. It was physically impossible for 600,000 men to protect a frontier that ran from the mouth of the Rhine to the Black Sea and then on to the borders of the Persian kingdom in the east.

More men seemed the obvious answer—or a technological revolution, and that raises the critical point. It was in a sense misleading when I noted that we throw a far greater proportion of our manpower into battle in an emergency. When we do that, our whole civilian life is at once readjusted, not merely by austerity programmes and general belt-tightening, but also by increasing the *per capita* production of those (including women) who remain on the farms and in the factories. And that no ancient people could do because their technology was too primitive, resting almost entirely on the muscles of men and beasts; and because most of the population, the free as well as the half-free *coloni* and the slaves, had nothing to sacrifice to an austerity programme to begin with. Furthermore, the modern comparison fails for still another reason. Contemporary states have been able to make these extraordinary efforts for a limited time, on the assumption that the war will end soon enough. But this was not the Roman problem. They were not engaged in a war in that sense but were undergoing a persistent hammering, and it is pointless to talk about tightening the belt and working overtime seven days a week for a period of 200 years.

The Roman position can be presented in a simple model. With the stabilization of the empire and the establishment of the *pax Romana* under Augustus, a sort of social equilibrium was created. Most of the population, free or unfree, produced just enough for themselves to exist on, at a minimum standard of living, and enough to maintain a very rich and high-living aristocracy and urban upper class, the court with its palace and administrative staffs, and the modest army of some 300,000. Any change in any of the elements making up the equilibrium—for example, an increase in the army or other non-producing sectors of the population, or an increase in the bite taken out of the producers through increased rents and taxes—had to be balanced elsewhere if the equilibrium were to be maintained. Otherwise something was bound to break. Stated the other way round, if the boundaries of the Roman Empire had been at the ends of the earth, so that there were no frontiers to defend, and if the court and the aristocracy had been content to keep its numbers and its level of consumption unchanged, then there was no obvious reason why the Roman Empire should not have gone on indefinitely.

But of course none of the 'ifs' happened. The parasitic classes (and I use the word in its strictly economic sense with no moral judgments implied) kept growing larger, with the triumph of Christianity an important contributing factor after Constantine. So did the pressures on the frontier. A larger military establishment and more frequent battles in turn meant greater demands on the peasantry who made up the bulk of the population in this fundamentally agrarian world. With their primitive technology, there came a time when they could no longer respond, whatever their will may have been in the matter.

As the final insult in this tale of frustration, the population was apparently not even able to reproduce itself any longer. This is a difficult subject because we lack figures. Yet there are signs of some decline in the total population, at least from the time of Marcus Aurelius, the reign we keep returning to as the pivot. The surest sign is the increasing frequency of abandoned farmland, in Italy, North Africa, and elsewhere. In an age without technological advances, occupation of the soil is a gauge of the movement of population. When the population is going up, marginal lands have to be brought into cultivation, and then they are abandoned when the curve goes down. The documents of the period make it clear that manpower shortage was a problem, and a recognized problem, particularly in agriculture. The efforts of landed magnates to keep their peasants out of the army played a greater part in the military manpower difficulties than the occasional young man who chopped off his fingers. And the peasants, in their turn, showed a tendency to flee from the land into the cities or to become outlaws.

Decline in the birth-rate is a mysterious business. I know no satisfactory explanation for it in the Roman Empire. Some historians have tried to blame it on the low life-expectancy of the time, but an equally low life-expectancy was the rule everywhere until the nineteenth century, and still is in large parts of Asia, and we all know about the explosions in their population. I find the same difficulty with Professor Jones's suggestion that the peasantry had become too poor and too starved to rear children. I doubt if they were hungrier than the peasants of modern India or Egypt; and the upper classes, who ate far too much for their own good, did not seem to be breeding at a satisfactory rate either.

Whatever the explanation, the word 'depopulation' is too strong. It overstates the situation. Manpower shortage is a relative term. All resources—and manpower is another resource—are, or are not, sufficient not by some absolute measuring-stick but according to the demands made on them and the conditions of their employment. In the later Roman Empire manpower was part of an interrelated complex of social conditions, which, together with the barbarian invasions, brought an end to the empire in the west. The army could not be enlarged because the land could not stand further depletion of manpower; the situation on the land had deteriorated because taxes were too high; taxes were too high because the military demands were increasing; and for that the German pressures were mainly responsible. A vicious circle of evils was in full swing. Break into it at any point: the final answer will be the same provided one keeps all the factors in sight all the time.

I concede that this is neither a dramatic nor a romantic way to look at one of the great cataclysms of history. One could not make a film out of it. But it provides the necessary underpinning for the military and constitutional history and the magnificent moralizing of Gibbon. The Roman Empire was people and institutions, not just emperors, degenerate or otherwise. And it was the inflexible institutional underpinning, in the end, which failed: it could not support the perpetual strains of an empire of such magnitude within a hostile world.

XIII

AULOS KAPREILIOS TIMOTHEOS, SLAVE TRADER

AULOS KAPREILIOS TIMOTHEOS does not appear in any history book. There is no reason why he should, but an accident of archaeology makes him a figure of some curiosity if not importance. He was a slave in the first century of our era who obtained his freedom and turned to slave dealing, an occupation in which he prospered enough to have an expensive, finely decorated marble tombstone seven feet high. The stone was found at the site of the ancient Greek city of Amphipolis on the Strymon river, sixty-odd miles east of Salonika on the road to the Turkish border—and nothing like it exists on any other surviving Greek or Roman tombstone, though by now their number must be a hundred thousand or more. The stone has three sculptured panels: a typical funeral banquet scene at the top, a work scene in the middle, and a third showing eight slaves chained together at the neck, being led along in a file, accompanied by two women and two children who are not chained and preceded by a man who is obviously in charge, perhaps Timotheos himself for all we know. The inscription in Greek reads simply: "Aulos Kapreilios Timotheos, freedman of Aulos, slave trader."

It is not his occupation that makes Timotheos a rare figure, but his publicly expressed pride in it. The ancient world was not altogether unlike the southern United States in this respect. After the Civil War a southern judge wrote: "In the South the calling of a slave trader was always hateful, odious, even among the slaveholders themselves. This is curious, but it is so." More than two thousand years earlier a character in Xenophon's *Symposium* said to Socrates: "It is poverty that compels some to steal, others to burgle, and others to become slavers." In neither case was the moral judgment quite so simple or so universally accepted as these statements might seem to suggest, nor was it carried to any practical conclusion, for the most respectable people depended on these same "hateful" men to provide them with the slaves without whom they could not imagine a civilized existence to be possible.

Yet contempt of the slaver was not uncommon, and this suggests that slavery itself was a little problematical, morally, even when it was taken most for granted. On this score ancient and modern slavery cannot be wholly equated. There were special circumstances in the southern states, pulling in contradictory directions. On one hand slavery was 'the peculiar institution' and few southerners could have been unaware of the fact that most of the civilized world had abolished the practice and did not like it; whereas Greeks and Romans had no such external voice of conscience to contend with. On the other hand southern slaveowners found comfort in the colour of their chattels and in its concomitant, the belief in the natural inferiority of black men— a defence mechanism of which the ancients could make relatively little use. The Negro in the old South could never lose the stigma of slavery, not even when, as an exception, he was freed or, as was often the case, when he had some white ancestry. But the descendants of an Aulos Kapreilios Timotheos could become ordinary free inhabitants of the Roman Empire, wholly indistinguishable from millions of others.

We have no clue to Timotheos's nationality. His first two names were those of his master (Aulus Caprilius in Latin), which he took upon receiving his freedom, according to Roman practice. Timotheos was his name as a slave—a common Greek name that tells us nothing about him, since slaves rarely bore their 'own' names but those given them by their masters. In more primitive times the Romans usually called their slaves Marcipor and Lucipor and the like—that is, 'Marcus's boy' or 'Lucius's boy'—but soon they became too numerous and required individual names so that Marcus's slaves could be distinguished from one another. When that happened there was no limit to the possibilities. The choice was a matter of fashion or of personal whim, though one rough rule of thumb was applied with some consistency. As Roman power spread to the east, the empire was divided into a Greek-speaking half and a Latin-speaking half, and the naming of slaves tended to follow this division. It is more likely therefore that Timotheos came from the lower Danube, or the south Russian steppes, or perhaps the highlands of eastern Anatolia, than from Germany or North Africa.

To a buyer this question of nationality was important. It was generally believed that some nationalities made better slaves than others, temperamentally and vocationally. Prices varied accordingly, and Roman law (and probably Greek law, too) required the seller to state his chattel's origin specifically and accurately.

One example is worth looking at. In the year A.D. 151 a Greek from Alexandria purchased a girl in the market in Side, a city on the south coast of Anatolia (about two hundred miles west of Tarsus) that had a long tradition and notoriety as a centre of slaving activity. He took the girl back to Egypt with him, and also the bill of sale—a bilingual document in Greek and Latin, written on papyrus, which was found in legible condition at the end of the nineteenth century. The girl is described in this way: "Sambatis, changed to Athenais, or by whatever other name she may be called, by nationality a Phrygian, about twelve years of age . . . in good health as required by ordinance, not subject to any legal charge, neither a wanderer nor a fugitive, free from the sacred disease [epilepsy].'' The seller guaranteed all this under oath to the gods Hermes and Hephaestus, and under penalty of returning the price twice over should any of it be untrue. The phrase "or by whatever other name she may be called" is a typical lawyer's escape clause; in fact, the girl was born free and given a good Phrygian name, Sambatis, which was replaced by the Greek name Athenais when she was enslaved. How this happened cannot be determined, but it was well known in antiquity that Phrygians often sold their own children into captivity, a practice they continued even after Phrygia was incorporated into the Roman Empire. It is also not stated whether the buyer and seller were professional slave dealers, but Side was a long way to come from Egypt merely to purchase one little girl for oneself.

Bills of sale were usually written on perishable material, so that it is only by accident that a handful, written on papyrus or wax tablets, have survived. This is a pity, because there is no other evidence from which to build a statistical picture of the racial and national composition of the large slave populations of the ancient world. But the broad contours of the picture are clear enough, and they shifted with the times. The crucial point was that there were no specifically slave races or nationalities. Literally anyone and everyone might be enslaved, and which groups predominated at one time or another depended on politics and war. Greeks enslaved Greeks when they could, Romans enslaved Greeks, and they both enslaved anyone else they could lay their hands on by capture or trade.

The majority of slaves, however, were always 'uncivilized' from the point of view of the Greeks and Romans. In principle the slave is an outsider, a 'barbarian', and that sets him apart from all the other forms of involuntary labour known to history—from the Egyptian peasants who were conscripted to build the pyramids, from the *clientes* of early

Rome, from debt-bondsmen, serfs or peons. The slave is brought into a new society violently and traumatically, uprooted not only from his homeland but from everything which under normal circumstances provides human beings with social and psychological support. He is torn from his kin, from his fellows, from his religious institutions, and in their place he is given no new focus of relations other than his master, and, in a very unreliable way, his fellow slaves. Nor can he expect support from other depressed groups within the new society to which he has been transported. He has lost control not only over his labour but also over his person (and his personality). Hence free sexual access to slaves is a fundamental condition of slavery, with complex exceptions in the rules regarding access of free females to slave males.

Inevitably the Greeks and Romans also made the attempt to justify slavery as an institution on the ground of the natural inferiority of the slaves. The attempt failed: it had to for several reasons. In the first place, there was too large a minority that could not be squeezed into the theory. For example, after the Romans defeated the Carthaginians under Hannibal, they turned east and conquered the Greek world, bringing back to Italy in the course of the next two centuries hundreds of thousands of captives. Among the effects of this involuntary Greek invasion was a cultural revolution. "Captive Greece made captive her rude conqueror," said the Roman poet Horace, and it was manifestly impossible to maintain the doctrine of natural inferiority (which might do for Germans) against a people who provided the bulk of the teachers and who introduced philosophy and the drama and the best sculpture and architecture into a society whose virtues had not previously lain in those directions.

In the second place, it was a too frequent practice in antiquity to free one's slaves as a reward for faithful service, most often, perhaps, on one's deathbed. There were no rules

about this, but some idea of the proportions that were sometimes reached can be gathered from one of the laws passed by
the first of the Roman emperors, Augustus. He tried to put a
brake on deathbed manumissions, probably to protect the
interest of the heirs, and so he established maxima on a sliding
scale, according to which no one man was allowed to free
more than one hundred slaves in his will. After centuries of
continuing manumission, who could distinguish the 'naturally
superior' from the 'naturally inferior' among the inhabitants
of Greek and Roman cities (especially in the absence of any
distinction in skin colour)?

Human nature being what it is, many individual slaveowners
no doubt went right on wrapping themselves in their pre-
ordained superiority. But as an ideology the notion was
abandoned, and in its place there developed one of the most
remarkable contradictions in all history. "Slavery," wrote
the Roman jurist Florentinus, "is an institution of the law of
all nations whereby someone is subject to another *contrary to
nature*." That definition became official: we find it enshrined
in the great codification of the law by the emperor Justinian,
a Christian emperor, early in the sixth century. Yet no one,
at least no one of consequence, drew the seemingly obvious
conclusion that what was contrary to nature was wrong and
ought to be abolished.

War was the key to the whole operation. The ancient
world was one of unceasing warfare, and the accepted rule
was that the victor had absolute rights over the persons and
property of his captives, without distinction between soldiers
and civilians. This right was not always exercised in full
measure; sometimes tactical considerations or pure magnani-
mity intervened, and sometimes more money could be raised
by ransom than by sale into slavery. But the decision was the
victor's alone, and a graph would show no more than occasional

downward dips in the curve, never a long period (say fifty years) in which fairly large numbers of captives were not thrown onto the slave market. No total figures are available, but there can be no doubt that in the thousand years between 600 B.C. and A.D. 400, the Greeks and Romans between them disposed of several million men, women and children in this way.

This is not to say that wars were normally undertaken simply as slave raids, though some surely were—as when Alexander the Great's father, King Philip II of Macedon, deliberately undertook an expedition into the Scythian regions north of the Black Sea in order to replenish his depleted treasury in 339 B.C. He is said to have brought back 20,000 women and children along with much other wealth. Granted that this was not a typical affair and that wars usually had other causes, it remains true that the prospect of booty, among which slaves bulked large, was never absent from the calculations—partly to help maintain the army in the field, always a difficult problem in antiquity, but chiefly to enrich both the state and the individual commanders and soldiers. Caesar went off to Gaul an impoverished nobleman; he died a multimillionaire, and Gallic captives played no small part in bringing about this change of fortune. When he took the town of the Atuatuci (probably Namur), he himself reported that 53,000 were sold off; and after the battle of Alesia in 52 B.C. he gave one captive to each of his legionnaires as booty. Yet Caesar did not plunder to the limit; he often tried conciliatory tactics in the hope of dividing the Gallic tribes, as he did after Alesia when he restored 20,000 captives to the Aedui and Arverni. A century earlier 150,000 Epirotes from seventy towns in north-western Greece had been sold off by the Roman state because they had supported the Macedonian king, Perseus, with whom the Romans were at war.

The figure 150,000 may be exaggerated, but human plunder

even in quantities only half that size created problems for an army on the march. It could become completely bogged down, and sometimes in fact it was. In 218 B.C. King Philip V of Macedon invaded Elis in the north-western Peloponnese and soon found himself so overburdened with booty, which included more than 5,000 captives and masses of cattle, that his army, in the words of the historian Polybius, was rendered "useless for service". He therefore had to change his plans and march through difficult terrain to Heraea in Arcadia, where he was able to auction off the booty.

This case is not typical. If it were, the military and therefore the political history of the ancient world would have been an altogether different one. Normally preparations were made beforehand for booty disposal, and they consisted above all in seeing to it that a crowd of peddlers and merchants came along, equipped with ready cash and means of transport. The booty was assembled at a designated spot and auctioned off (the Spartans, with their characteristic bluntness, gave the responsible officers the title of 'booty-sellers'). What happened thereafter was the sole concern of the buyers, and the army was free to continue on its way, enriched by the proceeds.

Possibly the scene on the tombstone of Aulos Kapreilios Timotheos represents just such a situation, the removal on foot of slaves he had bought at an army sale. Certainly this would have been a very profitable business (providing the wherewithal for an expensive marble memorial), for slaves and other booty must have been extremely cheap to buy under such conditions. The only flaw was that war, for all its frequency, was nevertheless irregular and could not guarantee a steady flow of merchandise, and other sources had to be tapped as well. One of these was 'piracy', an unfortunate label because it evokes the image of isolated Captain Kidds, whereas the reality was altogether different in scale and character: a continuous, organized activity, illegal yet (like rum-running) not unwelcome to many of its ultimate beneficiaries, the consumers. Among the Greeks even in classical times this was a traditional occupation in certain areas, especially in the western part of the Greek peninsula.

But that was small stuff compared with the later upsurge in the Roman Republic, beginning about 150 B.C. Then there arose in the eastern Mediterranean a complex business network of pirates, kidnappers and slave dealers, with its headquarters apparently at Side and its main emporium on the island of Delos (whose docks were rebuilt and extended so that it was possible to turn over as many as 10,000 slaves in a day). The main impetus to this traffic was the rise in Italy and Sicily of the *latifundia*, large estates or ranches owned by absentee landlords and worked by slave gangs. The profit-side of the trade left a mark on Delos that is still visible today in the excavated remains of the rich houses of the Italian traders.

Direct consequences of the trade were two of the greatest slave revolts in antiquity, both in Sicily—the first beginning before 135 B.C., the second a generation later at the same time as the invasion of Gaul by the Cimbri and Teutones. To meet that invasion, Marius was authorized to levy auxiliary troops wherever he could. When he appealed to Nicomedes of Bithynia (lying just east of the Bosporus), a 'client-king' under Roman suzerainty, Nicomedes replied that he had no men to spare because most of his subjects had been carried off into slavery by Roman tax collectors. The Senate was alarmed (by the Germans, not by the complaint) and ordered provincial governors to release any 'allied' subjects whom they found in slavery in their districts. Eight hundred were accordingly freed in Sicily, but this was an isolated action that hardly scratched the surface of the problem.

The needs of the *latifundia* owners were comparatively

simple: quantity rather than quality of labour was what they were after. But important as they were, they were not the only consumers. In 54 B.C. Cicero wrote to his friend Atticus that Caesar's second expedition to Britain was causing concern in Rome. Among other things, it was now clear that there was no silver on the island and "no hope for booty other than captives, among whom I believe you cannot expect any highly qualified in literature or music". The sneer need not be taken too seriously, but it does point to still another aspect of the slave procurement problem, the demand for specialist skills.

Slaves could be trained, of course, especially if they were bought young. All vocational training in antiquity was accomplished by the apprenticeship system, and slave boys or girls were often so taught alongside their free contemporaries. Gladiators were specially trained for their profession and obviously had to be, since no one was normally brought up from childhood with that aim in view. They were an exceptional group, requiring exceptional techniques that were developed in schools established for the purpose. Probably the earliest was in Capua, and it is no coincidence that Capua was the centre from which the gladiator Spartacus organized the third great—and the most famous—slave revolt in antiquity (73–71 B.C.).

There were limits to the training of slaves, however, quite apart from strictly economic considerations. The right raw material was a necessary pre-condition: in the case of gladiators, Celts, Germans and Thracians were sought, rather than Greeks or Syrians. Or in the case of the Athenian silver mines, the preference was for men with mining experience (Thracians and Paphlagonians), and the scale of the problem is shown by the fact that in the fourth century B.C. the concentration of slaves in these mines reached a peak of perhaps 30,000. What happened, then, if in any given decade war and piracy together slacked off or turned up mostly women and children?

In the year 477 B.C. or thereabouts the Athenians established a police force of 300 Scythian slaves, owned by the state and housed originally in tents in the public square—the Agora—and later on the Acropolis. The system lasted for a hundred years, and the number of men may eventually have been increased to a thousand. Now Scythians were famous as bowmen, an art little practised among the Greeks, and they were sometimes employed in this capacity as mercenary troops. But the Athenians did not hire their Scythian policemen, they bought them. How on earth did they get this curious idea? And how could they count on regular replacements to keep the force up to par?

The answer is that there was already in existence by 500 B.C. a regular trade in 'barbarians', who were bought from their own chieftains—captives in their own wars, children, human levies, and the like—exactly as most Negro slaves were obtained in more modern times. This trade had nothing to do with Greek or Roman military activity or with piracy. It was a purely private business carried on by traders who had their personal connections and methods in the various regions outside the Greco-Roman world proper. To return to Aulos Kapreilios Timotheos once more, it is likely that this was how he operated. Certainly the place where his tombstone was found was a main debouching point for traffic coming from the regions of the lower Danube into the Aegean Sea. Had he lived five hundred years earlier, the Athenian state could confidently have placed an order with him to supply fresh stock for its police force whenever needed.

As a commodity slaves created peculiar problems for the merchant. Apparently in the larger cities there were a few shops where slaves could be bought: in Rome in Nero's time they were concentrated near the temple of Castor in the Forum. But they were the exception. One could not keep on hand, like so much merchandise on the shelves, a supply of gladiators, pedagogues, musicians, skilled craftsmen, miners, young children, women for brothels or concubinage. The slave trade has always been conducted in a special way, and the ancient world was no exception. On the one hand there were the main slave markets where, probably on fixed dates, dealers and agents could count on large supplies being put up for sale. Some of the centres were the obvious larger towns, such as Byzantium or Ephesus or Chios, but there were important lesser markets, too, like Tithorea in central Greece where there was a slave sale twice a year on the occasion of the semi-annual festival in honour of the goddess Isis. On the other hand, itinerant traders went with their slaves wherever there were potential customers, to garrison towns, country fairs, and what not.

The actual sale was normally by auction. The only surviving pictorial representations are on tombstones again, to be exact on two—one from Capua and the other from Arles— with substantially similar scenes. On the Arles stone the slave stands on a rotating platform while a man, presumably a possible buyer, lifts his single garment to reveal his very muscular legs and buttocks, and the auctioneer stands nearby in a characteristic pose with his arm outstretched. As the Stoic philosopher Seneca observed, "When you buy a horse, you order its blanket to be removed; so, too, you pull the garments off a slave."

Seneca was one of the wealthiest men of his day, in an age (the first century A.D.) of enormous fortunes and luxurious living, and of course he possessed his quota of slaves. In one of his *Moral Epistles* he insists that a slave is a man with a soul like every free man; like you and me, he says. From this he concludes that one should live on familiar terms with one's slaves, dine with them, converse with them, inspire respect in them rather than fear—everything but free them.

Seneca was a Roman, but his attitude was more Greek than Roman. To the Greeks, as Nietzsche once remarked epigrammatically, both labour and slavery were "a necessary disgrace, of which one feels *ashamed*, as a disgrace and as a necessity at the same time". It would be more correct to say that the shame was generally subconscious; one sign was the almost complete silence of ancient writers about what was surely the ugliest side of the institution, the slave trade itself. The occasional exception usually has a special twist to it. Thus Herodotus tells a story about a dealer from Chios named Panionion, who specialized in handsome young boys whom he castrated and then sold, through the markets at Ephesus and Sardis, to the Persian court and other eastern customers. One of his victims became the favourite eunuch of King Xerxes; when the opportunity fell his way, he took the appropriate revenge on Panionion and his four sons. Herodotus applauded, for in his view Panionion "gained his livelihood from the most impious of occupations", by which he meant not the slave trade as such but the traffic in eunuchs.

This may seem a hairsplitting distinction, but distinctions have to be drawn. The ancient world was in many respects a brutal one by modern standards. The gladiatorial shows were surely among the most repellent of its habits—as the Greeks would have agreed until they, too, were finally corrupted by the Romans—yet there is abundant evidence that gladiators were proud of their successes and that not a few free men voluntarily joined their ranks. This, it can reasonably be argued, merely proves how deep the brutalization went. But what about the Paphlagonian named Atotas in the Athenian silver mines, who claimed descent from one of the Trojan heroes and whose tomb inscription included the boast, "No one could match me in skill"? The skill and artistry of slaves was to be seen everywhere, for they not only were used as crude labour in the fields but were employed in the potteries and textile mills, on temples and other public buildings, to perform the most delicate work. The psychology of the slave in the ancient world was obviously more complicated than mere sullen resentment, at least under 'normal' conditions.

Even the slave trade had its shadings, so that it can serve as a barometer of the state of the society itself. It is no coincidence that the last century of the Roman Republic, a period in which moral and social values broke down badly, was the period of the most reckless slave hunting and of the great slave revolts. Then came the relatively quiet centuries of the early Roman Empire, followed by the long period in which ancient society itself finally dissolved. One incident is symptomatic: when the Goths achieved a massive breakthrough into Thrace in A.D. 376, the Roman armies were badly handicapped because many of their officers were more interested in the profits of slaving than in resisting the barbarians.

But by then slavery itself was a declining institution, not as the result of an abolitionist movement but in consequence of complex social and economic changes which replaced both the chattel slave and, to a large extent, the free peasant by a different kind of bondsman, the *colonus*, the *adscriptus glebi*, the serf. Neither moral values nor economic interests nor the social order were threatened by these subtle changes in the status of the underlying population. Nor did slavery disappear from Europe altogether. The legal problems created by the continued existence of slaves required more space in the sixth-century codification of the emperor Justinian than any other topic. Philosophers, moralists, theologians and jurists continued to propagate a variety of formulas which satisfied them and society at large that a man could be both a thing and a man at the same time. The western world had to wait fifteen hundred years after Seneca for the radical final step, the proposal that slavery was so immoral that it ought to be abolished—and another three hundred years before abolition was brought about, by force and violence.

XIV

CHRISTIAN BEGINNINGS:
THREE VIEWS OF
HISTORIOGRAPHY

1 Allegory and Influence

WHO came first, Homer or Moses? That question was vigorously debated between Christian and pagan apologists in the last centuries of antiquity, and often it was turned into a blunter question. Who plagiarized from whom? As an anonymous writer of about the year 200 phrased it,

> I think you are not ignorant of the fact . . . that Orpheus, Homer and Solon were in Egypt, that they took advantage of the historical work of Moses, and that in consequence they were able to take a position against those who had previously held false ideas about the gods.

Among his many 'proofs' were the 'borrowing' of the opening of Genesis for one bit of the description of the shield of Achilles in the *Iliad*, the portrayal of the Garden of Eden in the guise of the garden of King Alcinous in Book VII of the *Odyssey*; and Homer's referring to the corpse of Hector as "senseless clay", copied from "Dust thou art and to dust thou shalt return".

There were Jewish precedents for this kind of nonsense, especially in the Hellenized environment of Alexandria, going back at least to the middle of the second century B.C. In one sense the motivation is only too obvious. Claims of priority are common propaganda in all sorts of movements: we have had some remarkable examples in our own day. But there was much more to it in the Homer-Moses debate. At that time Judaism and Christianity were unique in their exclusiveness. Conversion to either religion required the complete abandonment of all previous beliefs, whereas among the prevailing polytheisms one could add new gods or new rites to the old, or create new combinations. Only with the former is it proper to speak of conversion at all, and the psychological difficulties are enormous. In the year 200, for example, what happened to a Greco-Syrian from Antioch or a Greco-Egyptian from Alexandria who, in his adult years, was converted to Christianity, still very much a minority religion and a persecuted one to boot? Was he capable, emotionally and psychologically, of ridding himself totally of the Mother Goddess or Isis or Serapis, of all the associations which went with their worship, of all his personal experiences (even of his language) which had in one way or another been connected with these cults up to the moment of conversion? Could he tell himself that it had all been falsehood, super-stition and idolatry, and then wipe the slate clean?

There can be no wiping of slates, however much one may change one's intellectual position. Nor need there be, when there are so many other ways of adjusting one's past experi-ence to present needs. On the purely cerebral level, the priority argument offers one solution. Crude as it appears, it nevertheless attracted some of the most powerful of the apologists on both sides, Celsus and Porphyry, Origen and Tatian, for example. Another, more interesting and more satisfying, procedure—still on the cerebral level—is to resort to allegory (speaking broadly and somewhat loosely). Alle-gory is fundamentally a very simple device, and once one has learned the trick it has no limits, as Father Hugo Rahner's book *Greek Myths and Christian Mystery** reveals by massive examples. Although the book actually consists of a number of essays

* Translated by Brian Batteshaw (London: Burns & Oates; New York: Harper & Row, 1963).

previously published in German in various learned journals, it is an integrated whole. Its central theme is the translation and absorption of Greek myths into Christian mysteries: the myths of two magical plants, the moly and the mandrake, of the willow branch and of Odysseus and the sirens; the mysteries of the cross, of baptism, of the sun and moon, of the "healing of the soul".

Of course, neither the Hellenized Jews nor the Christians invented allegory as a rescue-operation. The Greeks already had a long tradition of this kind, and fundamentally for the same reasons. Although there was no question of conversion in their case, the more sophisticated Greeks, who could not accept the literal truth of the Olympic religion or of the accompanying myths, could equally not dismiss that central core of their culture, and so they allegorized it. The Stoics, in particular, went about doing so systematically, linking their explanations with their general notion of the brotherhood of man under God. However, their way of finding "hidden moral lessons in the myths of the ancient poet" is decidedly not to Father Rahner's liking. Stoicism is "enlightened scepticism", "smooth, plausible and supposedly self-evident", the "emptying of all religion". Of all the classical Greeks, Plato was the thinker who had the Truth "dimly intimated to him", namely, "the truth which is fundamental to all true therapy of souls, that man, if he is to be made whole and become a creature of light, must be guided by the over-whelming truth that comes from above—by the Logos himself."

When, therefore, the book opens (and closes) on the note, "We have become Barbarians and wish once again to be Hellenes," the word 'Hellene' must be understood in a very restricted, even one-sided way. It is not by chance that the idealization of Plato is accompanied by a total neglect of Aristotle. Father Rahner is a mystic. "Removed beyond the grasp of human wisdom" is the key phrase for the greatest of truths. Hence "we wish once again to be Hellenes" only in so far as there was a mystical side to Greek culture. And only in so far as it is recognized that even that Greek experience was "but a preparation".

> For all their wisdom, the Greeks could only express the goals towards which they were seeking to lead the soul in the form of myths. What they could not find words to convey was their intimation that a way existed. Only Christian interpretation would be bold enough to make its direction plainer and show that it led to Christ.

Again:

> The Church alone is in her own person an antiquity that still lives on with the full life of youth, an antiquity that will never be merely antiquarian. For she alone, through the light of the Logos, knows the measure of the heights and depths of the human soul. That is why she can discern the clear lineaments of truth which the Greeks only faintly apprehend.

None of this is arguable, or even discussable. Father Rahner may, and does, find a hundred ways to say the same thing; it always remains mere assertion. Either one accepts it or one is seduced by the fallacy of 'enlightenment' and does not accept it.

But Father Rahner's book is at the same time a serious historical account (published with extravagant claims) of an interesting and significant intellectual process, learned and heavily documented, and it is therefore legitimate to judge it by the accepted canons of historical writing. There is a vast literature on the interplay between early Christianity and Greek myths, Greek philosophy, Greek religion. Inevitably so, for, as the late Werner Jaeger wrote in his posthumous book, *Early Christianity and Greek Paideia*, "among the factors that determined the final form of the Christian tradition Greek civilization exercised a profound influence on the Christian mind." The historical question is about the nature, quality and extent of that influence and the ways in which it was transmitted. Jaeger is acknowledged to have been one of the most important students of the subject of our time, and it is at first puzzling to discover that Father Rahner virtually ignores his work in all his huge bibliographical apparatus. It is even more surprising to discover the total omission of Jaeger's Harvard colleague, Arthur Darby Nock, who also died in 1963, and whose hundred-page "Early Gentile Christianity and Its Hellenistic Background", published in 1928 and recently reprinted, has become a classic statement on precisely the question to which Father Rahner devotes his first, most critical and brutally polemical chapter. (I am unable to find a single reference anywhere to any of Nock's writings.)

In the end, the conclusion is imposed on the reader that it is not only 'the Greeks' and 'the Christians' whom Father Rahner defines one-sidedly, so as to exclude all men and all doctrines with which he disagrees or of which he disapproves, but that the whole of modern historical scholarship on the subject is treated in the same way. Such phrases as "the words of a profound scholar which represent the latest utterance on the subject" or "that most erudite and perceptive writer" must always be translated into "the writer or writing whose point of view I accept". With that key, we know how to interpret, for example, the assertion that "serious scholarship has passed its sober and, in the main, annihilating judgment" on the work of Richard Reitzenstein, perhaps the greatest authority of the early twentieth century on Hellenistic religion and mythology.

A comparison between the first chapter of this book and Nock's article is revealing. Both discuss the question whether or not in its early years Christianity borrowed in any significant sense from the so-called mystery religions of the Hellenistic world, with their mixed Greek and Near Eastern elements. Both answer firmly in the negative, Nock on the basis of a quiet, reasoned presentation of the evidence, Father Rahner by an angry rejection of the very idea that Christianity could have 'borrowed' at all.

> Christianity is a thing that is wholly *sui generis*. It is something unique and not a derivative from any cult or other human institution, nor has its essential character been changed or touched by any such influence.

He goes further. To insure his position, he grossly distorts the history and nature of the Hellenistic mystery religions, denying them any ethical content whatever until a date so late that, if anything, the influence would have had to be from Christianity to them and not the other way round. And he omits a third element from the picture altogether, and that is Judaism. Where Nock writes, about a particular Christian doctrine, that its roots are not Greek but that "the key . . . is given to us by Jewish conceptions alone", Father Rahner would say that its roots are not Greek—full stop. Nor is this omission restricted to the first chapter. It is pervasive. The non-knowledgeable reader must come away from the book with the firmly fixed view that the Christian apologists were the first and only ones to allegorize myths "guided by the overwhelming truth that comes from above—by the Logos himself". It would then astonish him to browse in the twelve volumes of the Loeb Classical Library edition of Philo Judaeus (born about 30 B.C.) and to discover vast quantities of precisely this kind of allegorizing (applied to the Old Testament as well) linked with the Logos or Divine Reason. I am not suggesting that St Paul, for example, borrowed from Philo, or even that he had read Philo (as later Christian thinkers indubitably did). But I suggest—and more than suggest—

that omission on such a scale becomes suppression and is unacceptable in an historical account.

It is one thing to insist on the originality of Christian doctrine; it is something else again to treat its history (or that of any other religion) as if it were nothing more than the history of a few ideas in a vacuum. When a man like Clement of Alexandria (born about 150) devoted so much of his attention to the Christian implications of the Greek myths, his concern was not just an interest in ideas as such but a profoundly psychological one. He had no alternative, first because of his own conversion and then because of his desire to convert others like himself for whom Homer was the beginning of wisdom and true culture. Father Rahner is by no means unaware of psychological issues: some of the chapters in this book were originally papers read at meetings of the Jungian Eranos group in Switzerland. Here too, however, his one-sidedness becomes quickly apparent. The moment phallic symbolism is suggested, even Jung is dismissed along with the historians of religion whose research provided Jung with the necessary raw material. Similarly, in the very long and interesting section on the folklore of the mandrake, the magical (as distinct from the symbolic) lore is given some space on the pagan side, whereas for the Christian side one gets merely a bibliographical reference to a rare German work published in 1671, and the reader is further warned off by inverted commas: "the 'Christian' side of this magic."

There is no need to multiply examples: they recur in every chapter and on every topic. In the prologue to *Gargantua*, Rabelais asked the allegorizers of his own day with simple irony:

> Do you honestly believe that Homer, when he wrote the *Iliad* and the *Odyssey*, had in mind the allegories which have been foisted off on him by Plutarch, Heracleides Ponticus, Eustathius and Phornutus, and which Politian has purloined

from them . . . [or that] Ovid in his *Metamorphoses* could have been thinking of the Gospel Sacraments?

Father Rahner's answer, I believe after spending much time with his book, is an affirmative one, though not in the literal sense. I see no other way to interpret the many phrases such as "the evangelical truth hidden in the Homeric myth". Indeed, I see no other way to explain the very existence of this book. For all the interesting material it contains, it is not history as that word is customarily understood, but a witness, a testimony of faith.

2 *The Primitive Church*

Maurice Goguel died in 1955, having been for fifty years professor at the Faculté Libre de Théologie Protestante of the University of Paris. During that long and very productive life of scholarship all his effort was concentrated on a century and a half of history, to A.D. 150 in round numbers. Such dedication, such apparent narrowness of range, such austerity of style and manner, such unwillingness to make concessions to readers—these are qualities we have been taught to think of as Germanic rather than French. Goguel himself quotes with approval a reviewer's remark that "M. Renan thinks too much of beauty and not enough of truth". And it must be admitted that there is not the slightest danger that Goguel's books will have the public success of Renan's *Vie de Jésus*, which ran into thirteen printings within a year of its appearance in 1863, followed by fifteen printings of an abridged popular edition the next year, and which has been translated into thirteen languages.

Yet Renan is the fountainhead of the tradition of which

Goguel is one of the greatest exponents. Like all originators, Renan had his forerunners, the seventeenth-century Bishop of Chester, John Pearson, the eighteenth-century Hamburg professor Reimarus, David Friedrich Strauss and others. But, as Goguel writes, it was Renan who "brought forward the problem of the life of Jesus in such a way that henceforward it was impossible to withdraw it from this leading position". By which he meant the dawn of modern critical *historical* study of the origins of Christianity. Goguel opens the first volume of his own masterpiece, *Jésus et les origines du Christianisme*, of which *The Primitive Church** is the third and final volume, with these words:

> This book is an historical work. Although it deals with a question which is of immediate interest for the Christian faith, I have not felt at liberty to treat it with a different method than that which is accepted by historians in general, the only method by which it is possible to establish the reality of the facts of the past.

Goguel was a believing Christian, I hasten to add, who towards the end of his life "felt himself more religious than Christian, more Christian than Protestant, and more Protestant than Lutheran". For him there was no possible conflict between "faith" and "facts of the past". His final two sentences make that clear enough:

> The forms and phrases by which a religion is transmitted must be regarded as nothing more than the symbolic expression of a spiritual reality. As that expression is of

* Translated by H. C. Snape (London: Allen & Unwin; New York: Macmillan, 1964). The three volumes were originally published between 1932 and 1947. The first volume appeared in English translation in 1933 (reprinted in two volumes in Harper Torchbooks in 1960) under the title, *Jesus and the Origins of Christianity*; the second, *The Birth of Christianity*, in 1953. The three together total more than 1,500 pages of heavily annotated text. I shall draw on all three as appropriate.

quite a different order from factual knowledge, the one cannot in any way confirm or invalidate the other.

How organized Christianity came into being, in other words, may be examined independently of its "spiritual reality". At the same time, it was Goguel's faith which was a driving force behind his fifty years of unremitting labour, and which, incidentally, puts 'dedication to scholarship' in its proper perspective. What distinguishes a Goguel (or a Georges Lefebvre studying the French Revolution) from Dr Dryasdust can be summed up in the word 'significance'. Even a Parsee or Shintoist or agnostic can agree that the origins of Christianity have significance—enough to warrant a lifetime of scholarship which, from the nature of the enquiry, can never sink to pedantry when pursued with the integrity, rigour and high competence of a Goguel (or of a Loisy or a Guignebert, the two other Frenchmen who immediately come to mind in this context, whose faith was far more problematical). And it is the significance and the integrity which triumph over the austerity of the presentation for anyone who wishes to ponder and to learn and not just to be reassured in his devotion.

What may be learned from Goguel cannot be summarized briefly. Among other things he provides a critical survey of the scholarship in the field, past and present. Then he analyzes the sources text by text, sometimes several times over as the different books of the Bible and other Christian writings cast light or confusion, as the case may be, upon the several problems. As an extreme example, the short second chapter of the present volume, 'The Deutero-Pauline Doctrines of the Church', has six subsections, respectively entitled 'The Epistle to the Ephesians', 'The Pastoral Epistles', 'The Synoptic Gospels', 'The Book of the Acts', 'The Fourth Gospel and the First Epistle of John', and 'The Apocalypse'. In one sense, therefore, the three volumes

constitute a series of many short monographs. Yet they add
up in the end to a very complex and exciting history of the
development of early Christian thought, experience and
practice from the life and death of Jesus to the "*first steps
towards an all-embracing organization and the origins of the
Roman primacy*" (my italics).

Running all through there is a single leitmotif.

> Jesus did not foresee the Church; he did not found it.
> But from his actions it took its rise. . . . Without Jesus
> the Church would not have been born, and yet Jesus did
> not even foresee the Church. What he desired and pro-
> claimed was not the Church but the Kingdom of God.
> Without Paul . . . it would not have presented the face
> which it has for us across nineteen centuries of history.
> And yet Paul had no intention to be a creator or even only
> an organizer; he did not feel that he was so; he only wished
> to be a witness. . . . The Christianity of the Church was
> the extension, stabilization and organization of a religion
> which had been that of Jesus. Jesus was not the founder
> and earliest representative of Christianity but its object.

At the end of the first volume Goguel said this in even more
lapidary fashion: "Did Jesus feel that he was bringing a new
religion to his nation? This question did not occur to him."

If so, how and why did a new religion and its appropriate
organization come into being? That is the theme, and for
Goguel the answer lies primarily in "spiritual causes". Though
he concedes that "the birth and growth of the Church, together with its adaptation to the accident of the environment,
are also sociological facts", he is really not much interested
in institutions or institutional history in the common sense of
those terms. He prefers "the psychological method". Jesus
had proclaimed the Kingdom of God; then came the Crucifixion and therefore failure; trust in Jesus was put under great
strain, from which his followers were rescued by their faith

in the Resurrection. His life was now turned into a sacred history and a new religion was born.

Sacred history always "resembles a myth" and "its elaboration involves a certain disregard for minute historical accuracy". (It should be observed that Goguel is by no means the most radical of writers in this respect: among believing Christians there are historians of the early Church who go very much further in their rejection of the historicity of most of the Biblical tradition.) Nowhere is there more difficulty than with the central episode, the Resurrection. "No fact was more important for the primitive faith . . .; yet, on no fact is the tradition so diverse and incapable of being reduced to unity." Goguel's explanation here as always is psychological: a combination of "appearances" to a select few plus "the needs of apologetic added to a spontaneous tendency for the tradition to assume a more material and concrete form". The tradition thus follows "a law of religious development" that the "myth-making function" must intervene at the stage "when the period of creativity comes to an end and one of consolidation follows".

Enough has been said to make it obvious why Goguel sadly anticipated that some would be "pained, and, indeed, scandalized, by what they regard as a lack of respect for the Christian tradition". It is not only in the backwoods of Georgia that the illusion remains that much of the New Testament is literally true as historical fact as well as "spiritual reality". An Oxford historian, Mr A. N. Sherwin-White, has recently insisted* that the life of Christ as told in the Gospels and the life of Tiberius as related by Tacitus or the account of the Persian Wars in Herodotus are all of a kind, subject to the same tests and having the same general aims. "Not," he adds, "that one imagines that the authors of the Gospels set to work precisely like either Herodotus or Thucydides." Not precisely? Not at all. He has forgotten

* In *Roman Society and Roman Law in the New Testament* (1963).

that the Greek verb at the root of 'history' is *historein*, to enquire, which is what Herodotus set out to do, and what the authors of the Gospels (or the apologetic writers and theologians) did not set out to do. The latter bore witness, an activity of an altogether different order. In R. G. Collingwood's justly famous dictum,

> theocratic history . . . means not history proper . . . but a statement of known facts for the information of persons to whom they are not known, but who, as worshippers of the god in question, ought to know the deeds whereby he has made himself manifest.

The real difficulty begins if one agrees with Collingwood. Once the existence of a process of myth-making is accepted, the question is, How does one make a history out of such historiographically unpromising materials? There are no others. A handful of sentences in pagan writers, wholly unilluminating, and a few passages in Josephus and the Talmud, tendentious when they are not forgeries, are all we have from non-Christian sources for the first century or century and a half of Christianity. It is no exaggeration to say that they contribute nothing. One must work one's way as best one can with the Christian writings, with no external controls. Goguel's way, if I may oversimplify, is first to sort the traditions into strands (or to demonstrate that there was no early tradition at all if that was the case) and then to apply logical and psychological tests. One simple example will suffice. When asked by the Pharisees for "a sign from Heaven", Jesus replied, "There shall be no sign given unto this generation" (Mark VIII, 11-12). Goguel comments:

> This saying is certainly authentic, for it could not have been created by primitive Christianity which attached a great importance to the miracles of Jesus. . . . This leads us to think that Jesus did not want to work marvels, that is to say, acts of pure display.

It follows that stories like those of Jesus walking on water are "extremely doubtful". His healing, on the other hand, may be accepted, and, in conformity with the beliefs prevailing at the time, "it is true that these healings were regarded as miracles both by Jesus himself and by those who were the recipients of his bounty."

This application of the "psychological method" is neat, plausible, commonsensical. But is the answer right? Not only in this one example but in the thousands upon thousands of details in the story upon which Goguel or any other historian must make up his mind? I do not know what decisive tests of verifiability could possibly be applied. The myth-making process has a kind of logic of its own, but it is not the logic of Aristotle or of Bertrand Russell. Therefore it does not follow that it always avoids inconsistency: it is capable of retaining, and even inventing, sayings and events which, in what we call strict logic, undermine its most cherished beliefs. The difficulties are of course most acute at the beginning, with the life of Jesus. One influential modern school, which goes under the name of 'form-criticism', has even abandoned history at this stage completely. "In my opinion," wrote Rudolf Bultmann, "we can sum up what can be known of the life and personality of Jesus as simply nothing."

The difficulties do not stop with the death of Jesus. Not only did the myth-making process go on for a long time, but it was meshed in with the uncertainties, the gropings, and the conflict which characterized the early development of the Church. Goguel is right to stress the implications in this connection of the fact that the earliest Christian documents form a canonical collection: "What was remembered of the earliest days of Christianity passed through a kind of censorship so that there is only left for us what conformed to the doctrine of the church when it had become fixed in one single form." Much other material was in effect "thrown in the waste paper basket and disappeared". That is the other side of the coin of 'significance'. What was believed to be true about the origins of Christianity cut close to the bone. It still does. Thus, even the strictly scholarly debates, recently revived, about the responsibility of Jews and Romans, respectively, for the indictment and execution of Jesus, cannot altogether escape the practical significance of the answer over the next 1,900 years. Pilate, it is worth recalling, was canonized in the Abyssinian Church, his wife in the Greek Orthodox.

When the documents appear they immediately become tangled in the same network of uncertainties and prejudices. What have we learned from the Dead Sea scrolls, for example? One could answer that question with more confidence if there were any certainty as to what group the scrolls emanated from (a certainty which does not exist at the moment despite the emphatic assurance of much writing on the subject). Or consider the sensational Vatican excavations which uncovered St Peter's tomb. There is nothing in the archaeological evidence to indicate whether or not Peter's grave was also there: or even whether or not at the time the memorial was constructed Christians actually believed that they were marking the grave. The discovery of the tomb is therefore not incompatible even with Goguel's extreme scepticism about Peter in Rome. "And so it may be that Peter never came to Rome, or, if he came, he only played an obscure part there. He certainly did not found the Church; neither did he influence its development or determine its orientation." It need hardly be said that nothing else Goguel wrote is likely to be more abhorrent to many than this particular judgment.

Paradoxically, the validity in its broad outline of Goguel's general view of the origins of the Christian Church does not hang on the accuracy of his individual judgments. Nor need one accept the view wholly, and surely not the excessive psychologizing, to appreciate and treasure the effort. There is a first question to be put to any historical book: Does it stimulate reflection and bring one closer to understanding? *The Primitive Church* does.

3 *The Jews and the Death of Jesus*

It is hardly surprising to find some discordant notes among the general chorus of enthusiastic praise for the Second Vatican Ecumenical Council's declaration on the Jews. Thus, a Reuters dispatch from Damascus, under date of 5 December 1964, reported a protest at the Council sessions by the Syriac Orthodox Patriarch of Antioch and the Whole Orient. The Council's statement that the crucifixion ''cannot be blamed on all Jews living at the time indiscriminately, or on the Jews of today'', was totally unacceptable to Patriarch Ignatius Yacoub III, who said:

> The creed of the Church . . . is that responsibility . . . lies with the Jewish people until the world ends. The Bible, which recorded this creed, was not written for one generation, but for all generations.

Reuters did not say which passage or passages the Patriarch had in mind. Perhaps he isn't a very good Biblical scholar, and almost certainly he isn't much of a historian. But that hardly matters when he has so much history on his side— history in its meaning of 'that which has happened'. Whether a whole people may legitimately be held responsible for an event, past or present, is an interesting moral and theological problem—and sometimes a political problem, one with which our own age has been seriously troubled in quite a different context from that of the trial and death of Jesus. It cannot be denied, however, that, whatever the rights or wrongs, the notion of collective Jewish guilt has been a potent social force for nearly 2,000 years, and its doctrinal roots go all the way back to the Fourth Gospel. Why and how that should have happened is a complicated story which has little, if anything, to do with the answer to a different historical question, *Who Crucified Jesus?*, the title of a well-known book by Professor Solomon Zeitlin.*

There is a simple answer, of course. The Roman government crucified Jesus, through the instrumentality of its procurator in Judaea, Pontius Pilate. But that is too simple; one might even say simple-minded. The question raised in all four Gospels (in different degrees of intensity) is that of the role played by the Jews, and specifically by their leadership in Jerusalem, the high priesthood and the Sanhedrin. Was it they who were the prime movers, bringing so much pressure that the reluctant procurator finally agreed? The Vatican Council by implication accepts that view. The declaration 'absolves' the Jews as a collectivity, but not all Jews at the time, individually or institutionally. And, indeed, the Council could not have gone further without rejecting the Gospel accounts altogether. They are the sole source of information about the Passion—that cannot be said often enough or sharply enough—and all four agree on the responsibility of some Jews. Professor Zeitlin calls the latter Quislings, which is a neat way of turning the flank of the controversy, though the aptness of the analogy is not so certain as he makes out.

Judaea was a turbulent state. Autocratic rule had become habitual, first by the Hasmoneans, then by Herod and his family, and now by the Romans, none of them an attractive or lovable lot. The people were divided, bitterly, and it is

* Now reissued by the Bloch Publishing Company (New York).

characteristic of Jewish history in this period that class divisions and political conflicts were indistinguishable from sectarian religious disputes. Josephus is our main authority, and nothing could be more revealing than his persistent use of the word 'bandits' as a label not only for the outlaws who existed in considerable numbers in the mountains and deserts, but also for those who eventually brought about the great and unsuccessful revolt against Rome (ending in the destruction of the Temple in A.D. 70), among whom the Zealots seem to have been the main moving spirits. Now the Zealots were a traditionalist religious sect, who were as hostile to the Jewish aristocracy and high priesthood, for whom Josephus spoke, as to the Roman overlords. One must hold firmly to this sharp class conflict if one wishes to understand the age and its events. To say, with Professor Zeitlin, that "the Jewish people were crushed under Roman tyranny", is to miss that, and to fall into precisely the same trap as the collective-guilt argument. The class represented by Josephus did not feel tyrannized, or, at the very least, they accepted the Romans as an indispensable buttress for their own position; on the other hand, the 'bandits' were being tyrannized by high priests and kings long before the Romans took over.

Given that background, it is really a pseudo-question to ask whether the charge against Jesus was a religious one or political. The two were inseparable. It was perhaps possible (though unlikely) to be politically seditious without involving oneself in religious matters; it was wholly impossible to challenge the religious authority in any way without inviting the charge of political opposition—and there could no longer be political opposition which was not held to be seditious and punished accordingly. The early history of Christianity throughout the empire, not only in Judaea, is evidence enough, as are the complex shifts in the relations between

Christians and the Roman state until the Christians triumphed in the fourth century.

What, then, actually happened? Not even the Synoptic Gospels provide a clear and coherent account, and there are added confusions and impossibilities in the Fourth Gospel. There is one school of thought, to which I belong, which holds that no reconstruction is possible from such unsatisfactory evidence. Even if one could accept the view recently re-stated with much vigour by A. N. Sherwin-White in *Roman Society and Roman Law in the New Testament*, that the Acts and Gospels are qualitatively no different as historical sources from Herodotus or Tacitus, one does not get very far. Mr Sherwin-White has been able to demonstrate that the New Testament is very accurate in its details about life at the time, whether about geography and travel or the rules of citizenship and court procedures. Why should it not be? It is made up of contemporary documents, regardless of the accuracy of the narrative, and so reflects society as it was. That still does not tell us anything about the narrative details, and they are what matter. For that Mr Sherwin-White must, in the end, select and reject, explain and explain away, just as every other scholar has done for as long as anyone has felt the urge (and the possibility) of a historical reconstruction of the Passion.

One particular point of debate merits special notice. It is the Fourth Gospel in particular which raises it:

Pilate said, "Take him away and try him by your own law." The Jews answered, "We are not allowed to put any man to death."

Is that last statement true? Professor Zeitlin and others say it is not and that this deliberate falsification is the heart of the effort to transfer the onus from the Romans to the Jews. Had the Jewish leadership really wished to eliminate Jesus, the argument runs, they could have done so by the simple device of trying and executing him according to the law. There was no need to drag in Pilate at all. Against this, Mr Sherwin-White has produced powerful evidence that the one thing the Romans promptly abolished in their provinces was the right of native organs of government to pass sentence of death. This may have happened illegally from time to time, but the fundamental rule was unequivocal—and self-evident. He is probably right, but it still does not follow, as he seems to think, that the veracity of the Gospel narrative has thereby been substantiated, or even been made more probable in a significant sense.

Far be it from me to suggest, no matter how faintly, that it is ever unimportant to get the historical record right. But the feeling will not go away that there is an Alice-in-Wonderland quality about it all. There is something unhappily naïve about the implication that anti-Semitism might quietly disappear if one could only demonstrate decisively that no Jews, or just a few Quislings among them, shared in the responsibility for the crucifixion. When it comes right down to it, welcome as the Vatican Council's declaration must be, its practical significance is problematical. Collective Jewish wickedness permeates the whole of western culture. Are we to undertake a great campaign of elimination, beginning, say, with Bach's *Passion According to St John*, the words and music together? The dead past never buries its dead. The world will have to be changed, not the past.

XV

THE YEAR ONE

DECISIVE years, like decisive battles, are an old favourite with historians. Some—1492, 1776, 1914—are pretty obvious: knowledgeable contemporaries could not have escaped the feeling that something big was up, even though they could not have foreseen all the consequences. More often, however, great historical processes begin altogether invisibly, and only much later, looking back, is it possible to pin the critical date down. Such a year is the Year One. Indeed, of all the great years in history it is the oddest because no one alive at the time, or for centuries thereafter, had any idea that this was the Year One at all. If they ever used such a date, they would have meant by it the year in which the world was created, not what we mean by A.D. 1.

How, for example, was a birth certificate, a marriage contract, a business agreement, dated in the Year One? There is no single answer to such a question, since for most of the purposes of ordinary living, local dates were used. In Rome a contract would be dated "in the consulship of C. Caesar son of Augustus and L. Aemilius Paullus son of Paullus". Elsewhere there were regnal years, or years of local officials, or of priesthoods. This may look like chaos to us, habituated as we are to a continuous, fixed calendar in use more or less all over the world, but it worked well enough. Only the learned were troubled, the men who wanted an exact answer to the question 'How long ago?' or who wished to synchronize events in Greek and Roman history. A number of systems had been invented for their use. In Rome scholars commonly dated events from the legendary foundation of the city by Romulus in the year we call 753 B.C.; in Greece they used four-year units, Olympiads, beginning with the first Olympic

Games in 776 B.C. In those two systems the Year One was, respectively, 754 A.U.C. (*ab urbe condita*) and the first year of the 195th Olympiad. No system was official: every scholar and historian was free to choose whichever he preferred, singly or in combination.

It is therefore hardly surprising that it took the Christians a long time to think up and introduce a scheme of their own. The honour goes to an eastern Greek-speaking monk, Dionysius Exiguus, who lived in Rome in the first half of the sixth century. He calculated that Christ was born in 754 A.U.C., called that the first 'year of our Lord', *anno Domini*, and counted everything that preceded it as so many years *ante Christum*, 'before Christ'. His calculation was slightly inaccurate. The only real evidence is in two of the four Gospels, and unfortunately that is conflicting and irreconcilable. If Matthew is right in the way he dates the flight into Egypt, then Jesus was born in or shortly before the last year of the reign of King Herod the Great, who died in 4 B.C. But if Luke is right in linking the Nativity with a census—"And all went to enrol themselves, everyone to his own city"—then the date must be A.D. 6 or even 7. On neither account is A.D. 1 possible. Nevertheless, Dionysius's chronological scheme spread gradually, first in the west, more slowly in the east, until it achieved near universality. The Year One—whatever it really was—became a great year, for many the greatest year in all history.

If A.D. 6 is the right date, then Jesus was born in the newly established Roman province of Judaea. In that year the Romans deposed Herod's son Archelaus, took over Judaea, and sent in Syria's governor, Quirinius, with instructions to conduct the first census there. Galilee, on the other hand, was allowed to continue under the family of Herod for another generation. This rather confusing political situation was not untypical of districts on the eastern frontier of the Roman empire, where imperial policy fluctuated between backing local client-kings and ruling directly. After all, Palestine was a long way from Rome. Problems much nearer home were pressing: large forces were just then occupied with trying to incorporate the German territory between the Rhine and the Elbe. They were wiped out in A.D. 9 in a treacherous ambush by Arminius (Hermann), a German chieftain who had earlier served in the Roman auxiliary forces and been rewarded with Roman citizenship. That disaster in the Teutoburg Forest effectively settled the northern frontier of the empire on the Rhine-Danube line, subject to various later adjustments, including the conquest of Britain. The western frontier was the Atlantic Ocean; the southern was the Atlas Mountains, the Sahara, and the cataracts of the Nile—though parts of northern Africa had the same shifting political history as Judaea.

The Roman Empire was an empire in the strictest possible sense. The 'Roman people'—that is, Roman citizens who were concentrated very largely in Rome and central or northern Italy—ruled all the rest as subjects. The empire outside Italy was divided into what were called *provinciae*, which were not provinces in the way Ontario is now a province of Canada, but rather colonies in the way India or Nigeria were British colonies before they obtained their independence. The total area of the empire in A.D. 1 was nearly 1,250,000 square miles, the population perhaps 60,000,000. Whether anyone, in or out of government, actually knew the latter figure is much to be doubted. Although censuses were taken, they were irregular, and they came at different times in different provinces. Their sole purpose was to bring the tax rolls up to date: the tax collector, along with the soldier, was the most obvious and ubiquitous link between the provinces and Rome.

Rome had begun to acquire provinces as far back as the third century B.C., and the process never stopped until the second century of the Christian Era. Imperial expansion usually looks deceptive in its motivation because defence and strategy can so plausibly be adduced as the excuse: the farther the frontiers are extended, the farther the menaces—real or imaginary—are pushed back. But in antiquity in general, and among the Romans in particular, there seems to have been much less effort than in modern times to disguise or deny the open exploitation of empire. Whatever the reasons piously given for their conquest and incorporation in each individual instance, the right to profit directly from conquered lands was freely recognized. That meant not only taxes—in goods, services and money—for the state, but often great personal income, legal or illegal, for high officials and members of the tax-farming corporations. It was also in the interests of Rome that her empire be pacific and orderly, as well as reasonably well administered locally. To achieve the latter aim she depended chiefly on the local ruling classes, for she lacked the manpower to do otherwise, and they normally played the part assigned to them as a pro-Roman counter-weight in what could well have become a rebellious situation.

From the days when Rome first began to expand, her rulers had also adopted a policy of as much non-interference as possible in social and cultural institutions, although not so much from a broad theory or principle of toleration as from the much more elementary consideration, Why bother? Rome had no 'mission'—that myth was imposed retrospectively much later. She wished to rule successfully, and it was repeatedly demonstrated to her that minimum interference paid off—even though the Roman provincial governor retained virtually absolute power and did not hesitate to use it when he felt the need, including the imposition of the death penalty. Under normal conditions the upshot was that in their daily lives very large numbers of people were touched lightly indeed by Roman rule. That was particularly true in the eastern parts of the empire which had had a high civilization

of their own long before the Romans came. These areas remained very diverse, both among themselves and from the
west—about as diverse as they had been in their days of
independence. The calendar is fairly symptomatic, language
even more so. Latin was of course the official language of the
Roman state. But it was not the language spoken in the east
or even in some western regions such as Sicily and Libya.
There the ruling classes and the intellectuals tended to speak
and write and think in Greek, the rest in their native tongues
—in some places Greek, in others Aramaic or Egyptian or
whatever. Educated Romans were more or less fluent in
Greek, but their counterparts in the eastern provinces rarely
troubled to know Latin equally well. When Josephus—
Joseph ben Matthias, member of a Jewish priestly family,
highly educated, born and bred in Judaea—wrote his *Jewish
War*, a pro-Roman eyewitness account of the Roman capture
of rebel Jerusalem and the destruction of the Temple in
A.D. 70, his first version was in Aramaic, his second in Greek.

Josephus was a Pharisee, for whom the villains among his
own people were the Zealots, who stirred up and led the
revolt against Rome. His favourite word for the rebels is
'bandits', so that bandits, Zealots, and lower classes are virtually synonymous in his books. The mighty Romans needed
four years to quell the Jewish uprising—precisely because
social revolt, the desire for independence and sectarian
religious conflict were closely intertwined. This was an age
of lavish living among relatively few men at one end of the
scale, and extreme poverty among the many at the other end.
The Gargantuan banquet given by the freedman Trimalchio
in the *Satyricon* of Petronius is funny in the way it exaggerates;
the account caricatures, but it does not invent out of whole
cloth. The wealth of Herod the Great was a subject for never-
ending comment by Josephus. But the linen weavers of
Tarsus, skilled free craftsmen whose products were sought

after throughout the empire, could never afford the small fees charged for the acquisition of local citizenship in their own city.

Outside Judaea serious revolt was rare, for whatever reason. There was much unhappiness and much grumbling, but it takes more than that to make a lasting mark on the record: history tends to be the history of the winners, with the losers assigned the passive, largely unvoiced, faceless role of the people on whom the winners operated. Romans in the Year One were able to contemplate their position with much satisfaction. Not only were they the rulers of what they chose to believe was the civilized world, but they had emerged successfully from a long, desperately violent, and dangerous period of civil war. The republican machinery of government, led by the exclusive, oligarchical Senate—which had sent victorious Roman armies east, west, north and south and had carved out the greatest empire yet known—had broken down badly by the end of the second century B.C. Various attempts to mend it had failed, until Julius Caesar's great-nephew and adopted son, Octavian, finally replaced the old system by a monarchy—although the explicit terminology of kingship was carefully avoided and a republican façade reconstructed, with Senate, popular assembly, consuls, praetors and so on. But a façade is just that: its function is to conceal the reality behind it. In January of 27 B.C. the Senate formally ratified the position Octavian had won by arms and conferred on him a new name, Augustus, by which he has been known ever since. At the same time a euphemistic title was chosen for him, Princeps—before this a common Latin word which the dictionary defines as "the first, chief, principal, most distinguished person", hence lacking any of the undesirable overtones of *rex* (king). He was also Imperator, a military title he used often because it affirmed his special relationship with the base and guarantee of his power: the army, roughly half of it Roman citizens in the legions, the other half auxiliaries recruited chiefly in the less Romanized provinces.

Twenty-seven years later Augustus was firmly in control of an empire which he had considerably enlarged. Small stirrings of anti-monarchical sentiment were crushed, all lingering misunderstandings about the real nature of his rule removed. In 2 B.C. he had been given the title *pater patriae*, Father of the Nation, which recalled to Roman citizens the despotic authority of the Roman *pater* at least as much as paternal benevolence. He lived on to A.D. 14, with only one new honour to look forward to: his formal deification upon his death (like Julius Caesar before him). As important as these titular acquisitions were his open manoeuvrings to establish a royal dynasty: Augustus and no one else was going to choose his successor, and in the process he trampled on some of the most deeply rooted of Roman traditions. In 4 B.C. the Senate decreed that his two grandsons (and sons by adoption), Gaius and Lucius, should be designated consuls at the age of fifteen and that they should actually assume office when they were twenty. Each was entitled 'Princeps of the Youth'. This rigmarole was pure crown-princedom. In the Year One, Gaius, having become twenty, was duly elected consul along with his sister's husband, L. Aemilius Paullus. Then Augustus's luck ran out: Lucius died the next year, Gaius in A.D. 4. The sick, ageing emperor proceeded to adopt Tiberius, making it quite plain that he did so joylessly, and it was Tiberius who eventually succeeded him.

That Tiberius was able to take over smoothly and peacefully is a measure of the full extent of Augustus's success. Historians commonly and rightly call Augustus the 'architect of the Roman Empire'. In the days when imperialism was still a virtue and Roman imperialism the accepted model, he was regularly referred to with unmixed adulation. The pendulum has now swung back, though less for some, perhaps, than for others—E. M. Forster calls Augustus "one of the most odious of the world's successful men". It is hard to imagine anyone today reading without discomfort these lines*:

> And here, here is the man, the promised one you know of—
> Caesar Augustus, son of a god, destined to rule
> Where Saturn ruled of old in Latium, and there
> Bring back the age of gold : his empire shall expand
> Past Garamants and Indians to a land beyond the zodiac.

Virgil and Horace were the towering figures in the literary circle patronized by one of Augustus's closest and richest friends, Maecenas. (It was not for nothing that the very name of Maecenas became a common word in the languages of Europe.) Augustus thought of everything: public opinion was not to be neglected any more than finance, dynastic arrangements, food supply, or the army. Even the coinage was harnessed. When he was given the title *pater patriae*, for example, his chief mint, at Lugdunum (Lyons), began to issue silver coins carrying his portrait with the legend *pater patriae* on the obverse; on the reverse were his two young grandsons in togas, with emblems of priesthood and the legend, "Gaius and Lucius Caesar, sons [by adoption] of Augustus, consuls-designate, *principes* of the youth." Coins circulate rapidly, and public response was not slow. Poets picked up the theme; so did individuals and communities in dedicatory inscriptions on monuments.

Yet it would be a mistake to speak cynically of prostituted art. Neither Virgil nor Horace, who died in 19 and 8 B.C., respectively, nor the historian Livy, who in the Year One

* From *The Aeneid of Virgil*, edited and translated by C. Day Lewis (London: The Hogarth Press, 1952; New York: Doubleday, Anchor Books ed., 1953).

was still writing away on his vast epic history of Rome, had been bought in any real sense. Horace was the son of a rich ex-slave, while Virgil and Livy came from the propertied middle classes of northern Italy. These classes had suffered heavily in the civil wars, but now there was peace again—the *pax Augusta*—and great hope for the future, both for Rome and for the empire. With renewed greatness would come moral regeneration. This last was a favourite theme of Augustus, expressed in a stream of legislation designed to curb excessively wasteful personal living, licentiousness and depravity in the upper classes. They were to be called back, these upper classes—not to the freedom and power they had had in the Republic, but to responsible participation in the army and the civil administration under the Princeps. Augustus himself, according to his Roman biographer Suetonius, listened to poetry recitals and readings from history, and he even enjoyed them "provided they were serious and the author of the first rank".

Moral crusades are never easy to judge: standards, motives and realities are too much like icebergs. Certainly the visible part of contemporary behaviour looked rotten enough, even allowing for differences between ancient and modern values. The banishment at different times for sexual depravity of Augustus's daughter and granddaughter is proof enough. A number of men of high rank were exiled with the former as her accomplices; the husband of the latter, L. Aemilius Paullus (who had been the second consul in the Year One), was executed. There is thus something altogether mysterious about both affairs. There is no particular reason to whitewash either of the Julias, but it is hard to avoid the implication that dynastic palace plotting was a more important element in the picture. Conspiracy was henceforth endemic in the empire, and it is not unimportant that it touched the heart of the regime as early as the reign of the founder himself.

One of the younger Julia's co-victims was the poet Ovid,

sent off to Tomi (now Constanţa) on the Black Sea, where he was forced to live out the remaining ten years of his life, grumbling, whining, and begging in the most toadying terms for a reprieve which never came. In a sense Ovid sums up in his own career the great paradox of the Rome of his day. What had he done to warrant such severe punishment? As far as we know, nothing—or at worst something trifling. But ten years earlier he had written the *Art of Love*, and throughout his brilliant career—he was enormously popular— he belonged to a circle of poets and intellectuals who gave only lip service to the glories of the new reign while they exulted in their own individuality and, sin of sins, in the delights of love when the Emperor was demanding moral regeneration. The *pax Augusta* was enforced by a military despotism; the literary renaissance was expected to stay pretty much in line; the rule of law could be broken at the ruler's whim.

It was not the brutality that disturbed anyone. The list of Augustus's massive philanthropies, which he himself compiled for posthumous publication, included the sponsorship of eight monster exhibitions in which about ten thousand gladiators fought, the largest number on record. These were now the most popular type of public show in the Empire. If the theatre was the characteristic secular building of classical Greek civilization, the amphitheatre was its Roman counterpart. What critics of the imperial system (the few whose voices we hear) attacked was not its brutality but the arbitrariness and the sycophancy it bred, the inevitable conspiratorial atmosphere.

Yet there *was* a great cultural renaissance under Augustus. And there was peace throughout the empire most of the time, peace without political freedom as the Greeks had once understood it, even without freedom in the more limited sense men had experienced in republican Rome, but more continuous peace than the Mediterranean world had perhaps ever known.

The Roman and Italian response is well documented in literature and sculptured monuments, and is not hard to understand. But what of the 'provincials', the subjects, and particularly what of the great mass of them who were not local
magnates supporting Rome in return for benefits received?
Part of the answer, for the east in particular, is that they began
to worship Augustus as Saviour, Benefactor and God Manifest
(Epiphanes), just as they had deified a succession of Ptolemies,
Seleucids, and other rulers in the preceding centuries.
Among the Romans themselves divinity had to wait until his
death; in the meantime only his genius or *daemon*, the im-
mortal spirit within him, could have an altar. But the east,
with a different tradition, built temples to Augustus the god.

This ruler-cult should neither be underestimated nor mis-
understood. It was cult in the strict sense, difficult as that
may be to grasp today. At the same time it did not prove the
existence of widespread popular enthusiasm for the ruler as
a person, or of anything more positive than a recognition of
the facts of life. Power had to be worshipped, that was self-
evident: the power of natural forces, Fate or Fortune, the
many gods and goddesses in their multiple attributes, and the
great power on earth. To do otherwise was stupid and
brought certain punishment, even though rewards for proper
veneration were unfortunately far from guaranteed, at least
in this life. In so one-sided a relationship, in a world in
which there was little hope of material success for the majority of the free population (let alone the slaves), and in which
the earthly power was now pretty close to despotism, fear
rather than love was often the dominating emotion behind
worship, at best fear and love together. Religion became
increasingly centred on salvation in the next world, whereas
it had once been chiefly concerned with life in this one.

However complicated the psychology, emperor worship
was a binding force in the empire. The first manifestations

were more or less spontaneous, but it would be naïve to imagine that Augustus or his advisers and successors were unaware of the value of the institution. Particularly zealous to foster it were the petty tyrants and client-kings who depended on Roman arms for their very existence, among them King Herod of Judaea (who also, significantly, introduced the amphitheatre and gladiators into his realm). Herod thereby set off a delayed chain reaction with the most far-reaching consequences. Where there were already many gods, to add the emperor to the pantheon was easy. The polytheistic religions of the eastern Mediterranean had been adding, combining, and altering their divinities and their rituals for millennia. A small minority of intellectuals rationalized the system into one or another kind of universal religion, in which the individual gods and their cults were all manifestations of one God. Everyone else was more literal-minded, with a take-it-or-leave-it approach that permitted one to pick and choose. It was physically impossible for anyone to participate in the observances of all the divinities. A policy of *laissez faire* prevailed, provided only that no one blasphemed against anyone else's gods and that cult did not become entangled with political opposition or create an excessive amount of vicious public immorality.

The Jews stood apart. Many now lived outside Judaea: there were particularly large communities in Egypt and elsewhere in North Africa, smaller ones in Asia Minor and in Rome itself. In the Diaspora they had become very much Hellenized: parts of the Old Testament had been translated into Greek by the middle of the third century B.C. because few could any longer understand Hebrew. In Palestine, by contrast, Hellenization had been relatively negligible, restricted to small aristocratic circles and to certain districts. Yet wherever they were, Greek and other external influences left untouched the fundamental commandments:

Thou shalt have no other gods before me. Thou shalt not make unto thee any graven image. . . . Thou shalt not bow down thyself to them, nor serve them: for I the Lord thy God am a jealous God.

Once before, in the second century B.C., there had been grave trouble over this question, when the Jews under the leadership of the Maccabees had rebelled successfully against Antiochus IV Epiphanes, the Greek ruler of Syria and Babylonia. Now Herod was trying to repeat the same sacrilege. There was an outcry and he quickly backed down, in time to avoid civil war but not an abortive attempt to assassinate him.

In the next generations the Romans were thus faced with a strange and to them distasteful and even unintelligible situation, with a people who would not play the rules of the game as they were understood by everyone else, who worshipped one God, an exclusive, jealous God. Opposition to emperor worship was to the Romans not so much a religious issue as a political offence, *contumacia*, insubordination, civil disobedience. Augustus and Tiberius made no attempt to force matters with the Jews, and under their immediate successors official policy was inconsistent. But Roman officials in the provinces, and the local populations, for reasons of their own, were far less tolerant and cautious; there were flare-ups against the Jews, ostensibly over imperial statues, in Egypt as well as in Palestine. The Jews themselves were right to be nervous about it. Jewish 'extremists' played on these fears, and on social unrest, till finally they brought about the great revolt which the emperor Vespasian and his son Titus smashed in A.D. 70.

It is this complicated combination of motives and circumstances that explains why Jewish nationalism emerged and rebelled whereas Egyptian or Syrian or Greek did not, though widespread poverty, imperial taxation, and similar factors were equally present in these other areas. Economic misery and social unrest had long been turning people to religious

ASPECTS OF ANTIQUITY

salvation as the only promise for the future. In this instance
religion drove men to political action (as druidism may also
have done in Gaul in A.D. 21). To put the whole burden of
explanation on emperor worship would be wrong: religious
exclusiveness and alienness, in a world which otherwise found
room for all varieties of cult and belief, bred misunderstand-
ing, dislike, wild rumours, irrational hate, mob violence. It
cannot be doubted that the destruction of Jerusalem was a
popular measure, on the whole, with other peoples of the
empire. Imperial Rome triumphed for the moment, only to
discover that she was faced with the same problem under a
new name, Christianity—a religion which was just as fiercely
monotheistic and exclusive as Judaism, and even more dynamic in its proselytizing zeal. ''Render unto Caesar the things
that are Caesar's'' did not extend to worship of Caesar for
Christians any more than for the Jews.

Of course there were no Christians in the Year One. Not
even a hundred or two hundred years later could anyone have
foreseen how radically the balance was going to shift, that the
invincible Roman Empire would turn out to be transitory while
the still negligible Christian sect would one day bid for
universality. To emperors and ordinary non-Christians alike,
Christianity was a nuisance and no more. Early in the second
century, Pliny the Younger, governor of the province of
Bithynia, wrote to the emperor Trajan for advice on how to
deal with men and women denounced to him for being
Christians. ''I have never participated in interrogations of
Christians,'' was his significant opening remark, and his
long letter confirms his ignorance on the subject. To test
persons accused, he continued, he required them to call upon
the gods, to sacrifice before the imperial statue and to revile
the name of Christ—''none of which things, it is said, genuine
Christians can be induced to do.'' Trajan in reply agreed that
Christians must be punished, but ''they should not be hunted

out''. Roman emperors never took so casual a view of problems they regarded as really serious.

Trajan, incidentally, was the last Roman expansionist. He conquered Dacia, roughly modern Transylvania in the loop of the lower Danube, and created a new province there. Then he embarked on an absurd campaign against the Parthian empire, the heirs of the Persians east of the Euphrates River. He had fleeting success, but Hadrian—who followed him on the throne—immediately and unavoidably gave up the new eastern gains. All in all, the frontiers of the Year One were not far from the absolute limits of the Roman world, except for adjustments, a few conquests, and the final elimination of client-kingdoms as in Judaea. Roman contacts through trade were something else again. Luxury goods moved back and forth across vast distances, and with the products some information and more misinformation. Even though silk came overland from China (the middlemen living in what is now Chinese Turkestan), it may safely be doubted if anyone within the Roman Empire had ever heard of the early Han dynasty or that it was about to come to an end just then (actually in A.D. 8). Trade with India and even Ceylon was more direct and on a considerably larger scale, chiefly by sea from Egypt. Indo-Roman trading stations existed as far away as Pondicherry; there was a drain of Roman coins to India and still farther east. Yet the knowledge of Indian life and civilization scattered in Roman literature is thin and unreliable, showing little advance over the reports brought back from the campaigns of Alexander the Great several centuries earlier. Similarly, there was trans-Sahara trade, especially for ivory, but almost total ignorance of the African continent below the desert.

The peoples the Romans knew best were of course their neighbours, the Armenians and Parthians immediately to the east, and, more important, the Germans beyond the Rhine and Danube. The latter were illiterate, organized in loose tribal federations rather than in more advanced political systems, and constantly on the move, both because their relatively primitive agricultural techniques exhausted the soil rapidly and because from time to time they were driven by invaders, such as the later Huns, who swept across the eastern and central European plains. Germans and Romans were in constant contact, sometimes hostile but more often neutral or even friendly, exchanging goods and occasionally ideas. It is hardly surprising that these less advanced peoples envied the superior Roman material standards and tried to share them, which meant trying to come into the empire.

Whatever the cultural influences going out—and they are visible in such far-flung places as Taxila in the Punjab, or among the Celts of Britain—it is easy (and sometimes too tempting) to exaggerate the reverse process, except in religion. Astrology from Babylon, the god Mithras, and the old Zoroastrian dual principle of Light and Darkness from Persia spread rapidly through the empire. Again one must not exaggerate; apart from these examples, the great matrix of religious innovation was *within* the empire, in its eastern regions: Egypt, Syria and Palestine, Asia Minor. And, of course, in the end the triumphant contribution from that area in this period was Christianity.

All this outruns the Year One by centuries, and it must be confessed that it was a decisive year only by convention, thanks to the slight error committed by Dionysius Exiguus. Nevertheless, the victory of Augustus and the birth of Christ between them marked out paths for the future, the impact of which cannot possibly be overstated. It is a commonplace to say that European civilization (and therefore American, too) has three roots, Greek, Roman and Judaeo-Christian. But it has become a commonplace because it is so obviously true.

The Romanization of western Europe, for which the Augustan imperial settlement was essential, was one factor that eventually made the idea of Europe possible. The eastern half of the empire was fundamentally not Romanized, and in the end it broke away, from Rome and from Europe; but it produced and exported to Europe a second binding factor, a common and exclusive religion. These were not the only factors in subsequent European history, to be sure. In history, unlike biology, one must not ask too much of roots. They cannot explain everything. It is enough to understand how deep down they go and what they have contributed.

BIBLIOGRAPHICAL NOTES

For an introduction to Greek and Roman civilization, with good bibliographies, see M. I. Finley, *The Ancient Greeks* (London: Chatto & Windus, 1963; New York: Viking, 1963; Penguin, 1966); M. Rostovtzeff, *Rome* (New York: Oxford University Press, 1960; Galaxy Books ed. by E. J. Bickerman, 1965). *The Oxford Classical Dictionary*, 2nd ed., by N. G. L. Hammond and H. H. Scullard (Oxford: Clarendon Press; New York: Oxford University Press, 1970).

I   The Rediscovery of Crete
II Lost: the Trojan War

On Crete, see R. W. Hutchinson, *Prehistoric Crete* (Penguin, 1962); J. D. S. Pendlebury, *The Archaeology of Crete* (London: Methuen, 1939, reprint, 1964; New York: Norton, 1965); J. W. Graham, *The Palaces of Crete* (Princeton, N.J.: Princeton University Press, 1962). The most recent examination of the archaeological evidence, with a firm conclusion in favor of the "orthodox" date for the destruction of Knossos, about 1400 B.C., is M. R. Popham, *The Destruction of the Palace at Knossos* (*Studies in Mediterranean Archaeology*, vol. XII, Göteborg, 1970).

The best book on the Homeric poems is G. S. Kirk, *The Songs of Homer* (Cambridge: Cambridge University Press, 1962), also published in a shorter, less technical paperback version as *Homer and the Epic* (Cambridge: Cambridge University Press, 1965). On heroic poetry generally, see C. M. Bowra, *Heroic Poetry* (London: Macmillan; New York: St. Martins, 1952). The archaeological evidence is surveyed in Lord William Taylour, *The Mycenaeans* (London: Thames & Hudson; New York: Praeger, 1964). I have tried to give a picture of the world behind the Homeric poems in *The World of Odysseus* (London: Chatto & Windus, reprint, 1964; New York: Viking, rev. ed., 1965; Penguin, rev. ed., 1967); of the problems surrounding the traditions of the Trojan War in an article, followed by comments by G. S. Kirk, J. L. Caskey and D. L. Page, in *Journal of Hellenic Studies*, vol. LXXXIV (1964), 1–20 (available separately

in the Bobbs-Merrill Reprint Series in European History, no. E–66);
of the development of Greek historical consciousness in 'Myth,
Memory, and History', *History and Theory*, vol. IV (1965), 281–302.
The Achchijawa documents are fully discussed in O. R. Gurney,
The Hittites (rev. ed., Penguin, 1964), pp. 46–58.

On special topics see M. I. Finley, *Early Greece: The Bronze and
Archaic Ages* (London: Chatto & Windus; New York: W. W.
Norton, 1970); J. Mellaart, *Catal Hüyük* (London: Thames & Hudson, 1967); J. Chadwick, *The Decipherment of Linear B* (Cambridge:
Cambridge University Press, 1958; Penguin, 1961); H. J. Rose, *A
Handbook of Greek Mythology* (6th ed., London: Methuen, 1958; New
York: Dutton, 1959).

III   Silver Tongue

The phrase "quieter moral virtues" is from A. W. H. Adkins, *Merit
and Responsibility: A Study in Greek Values* (Oxford: Clarendon Press;
New York: Oxford University Press, 1960). Pindar's *Odes* have been
edited and translated by Richmond Lattimore (Chicago: University
of Chicago Press, 1947).

V   Socrates and Athens
VI   Plato and Practical Politics

The only complete study of the Athenian impiety trials is by E.
Derenne, *Les procès d'impiété intentés aux philosophes à Athènes . . .*
(*Bibliothèque de la Faculté de philosophie et lettres de l'Université de
Liège*, vol. XLV, 1930).   On various aspects of the background, see
H. I. Marrou, *A History of Education in Antiquity* (London: Sheed &
Ward 1956; New York: Mentor [New American Library], 1964);
F. D. Harvey, 'Literacy in the Athenian Democracy', *Revue des
études grecques*, vol. LXXIX (1966), 585–635; E. R. Dodds, *The
Greeks and the Irrational* (Berkeley, Cal.: University of California
Press, 1951); G. S. Kirk and J. E. Raven, *The Presocratic Philosophers*
(Cambridge: Cambridge University Press, 1957); M. I. Finley,
'Athenian Demagogues', *Past & Present*, no. 21 (1962), 3–24.

A translation of the letters attributed to Plato, with detailed
commentary defending their authenticity, will be found in G. R.

Morrow, *Plato's Epistles* (Indianapolis, Ind.: Bobbs-Merrill Library of Liberal Arts, 1962); contra, see L. Edelstein, *Plato's Seventh Letter* (Leiden: Brill, 1966). See generally M. I. Finley, *Ancient Sicily to the Arab Conquest* (London: Chatto & Windus; New York: Viking, 1968), ch. VII.

For the current discussions of Plato and politics, see R. H. S. Crossman, *Plato To-Day* (London: Allen & Unwin, 1937, rev. ed. 1959; New York: Oxford University Press, 1959); K. R. Popper, *The Open Society and Its Enemies*, vol. I, *The Spell of Plato* (London: Routledge & Kegan Paul, 1942, 5th ed. 1966; Princeton, N.J.: Princeton University Press), the revised edition of which includes a reply to criticisms, notably by R. B. Levinson, *In Defense of Plato* (Cambridge, Mass.: Harvard University Press, 1953); R. Bambrough, ed., *Plato, Popper and Politics* (Cambridge: Heffer; New York: Barnes & Noble, 1967).

VII   Diogenes the Cynic

The largest collection of sayings attributed to Diogenes will be found in the unreliable *Lives of Philosophers* by Diogenes Laertius, written probably in the earlier part of the third century of our era. The papyrus containing Cynic diatribes was published in *Museum Helveticum*, vol. XVI (1959), 77–139. For two very different accounts of Cynicism, see D. R. Dudley, *A History of Cynicism* (London: Methuen, 1937); R. Höistad, *Cynic Hero and Cynic King* (Uppsala, 1948).

VIII   *Etruscheria*
IX   The Etruscans and Early Rome

Much the best introduction to the Etruscans is M. Pallottino, *Etruscologia* (originally published in 1942 and regularly revised thereafter); an English translation of the 3rd edition, by J. A. Cremona, was published by Penguin Books in 1955 but has been out of print for several years. A new edition is now in preparation. The Pyrgi tablets were published with a very full commentary in *Archeologia classica*, vol. XVI (1964), 49–117. For a guide to the voluminous and complex polemics on early Rome, see A. Momigliano, 'An Interim Report on the Origins of Rome', *Journal of Roman Studies*, vol. LIII (1963), 95–121; Fondation Hardt, Entretiens XIII, *Les Origines de la république romaine* (Vandoeuvres-Genève, 1966). Perhaps the best available work on Etruscan art is G. A. Mansuelli, *Art of Etruria and Early Rome* (New York: Crown, 1965; London: Methuen, Art of the World series, 1966); on Carthage, B. H. Warmington, *Carthage* (Penguin, 1964).

X   The Silent Women of Rome

The epitaph is quoted from R. Lattimore, *Themes in Greek and Latin Epitaphs* (Urbana, Ill.: University of Illinois Press, 1942, reprint, 1962).

XI   The Emperor Diocletian
XII   Manpower and the Fall of Rome

The standard work on the later Roman Empire is now A. H. M. Jones, *The Later Roman Empire 284–602* (3 vols., Oxford: Blackwell; Norman, Okla.: University of Oklahoma Press, 1964). The best introduction to Diocletian will be found in A. H. M. Jones, *Constantine and the Conversion of Europe* (London: English Universities Press, 1948; New York: P. F. Collier, Inc., 1962), and in the chapters by H. Mattingly, N. H. Baynes and W. Ensslin in the *Cambridge Ancient History*, vol. XII (Cambridge: Cambridge University Press, 1939). Selections in translation of the 'edict on prices' are published in Tenney Frank, ed., *An Economic Survey of Ancient Rome*, vol. V, *Rome and Italy of the Empire* (Baltimore, Md.: Johns Hopkins Press, 1940; reprint Paterson, N.J.: Pageant Books, 1959). The anonymous *De rebus bellicis* has been edited with translation and commentary by E. A. Thompson, *A Roman Reformer and Inventor* (Oxford: Clarendon Press; New York: Oxford University Press, 1952). On Diocletian's persecution of the Christians, see also G. E. M. de Ste. Croix, 'Aspects of the "Great" Persecution', *Harvard Theological Review*, vol. XLVII (1954), 75–113; W. H. C. Frend, 'The Failure of the Persecutions', *Past & Present*, no. 16 (1959), 10–30.

XIII   Aulos Kapreilios Timotheos

The monument was first published by J. Roger in *Revue archéologique*, 6th ser., vol. XXIV (1945), 49–51. The bill of sale quoted in the text will be found in *Fontes iuris romani antejustiniani*, vol. III, *Negotia*, ed. V. Arangio-Ruiz (Florence: Barbèra, 1943), no. 133. For a bibliography on ancient slavery see the analytical essay at the end of M. I. Finley, ed., *Slavery in Classical Antiquity* (Cambridge: Heffer; New York: Barnes & Noble, 1960, reprint 1968 with bibliographical supplement to 1967).

XIV   Christian Beginnings

Of Albert Loisy's many works, see, for example, *The Birth of the Christian Religion* (London: Allen and Unwin, 1948; New Hyde Park, N.Y.: University Books, 1962); of Charles Guignebert's, *Jesus* (London: Kegan Paul, 1935; New Hyde Park, N.Y.: University Books, 1956) and *The Jewish World in the Time of Jesus* (London: Kegan Paul, 1939; New Hyde Park, N.Y.: University Books; 1959). A. D. Nock's 'Early Gentile Christianity and Its Hellenistic Background' has been reprinted in a volume under that title, with a new introduction and two additional essays (New York: Harper Torchbooks, 1964); see also his *Conversion* (New York and London: Oxford University Press, 1933, paperback reprint, 1961). Also quoted in the text are R. G. Collingwood, *The Idea of History* (Oxford: Clarendon Press, 1946, reprint, 1966; New York: Oxford University Press, 1966); A. N. Sherwin-White, *Roman Society and Roman Law in the New Testament* (Oxford: Clarendon Press; New York: Oxford University Press, 1963).

Perhaps the best statement of the view that the Biblical account of the crucifixion is a deliberate attempt to transfer the onus from the Romans to the Jews will be found in Paul Winter, *On the Trial of Jesus* (Berlin: De Gruyter, 1961). For a full account of the ancient uses of allegory, including material on the Homer-Moses debate, see Jean Pépin, *Mythe et allégorie, Les origines grecques et les contestations judéo-chrétiennes* (Paris: Aubier, 1958). Also valuable are Johannes Weiss, *Earliest Christianity: A History of the Period* A.D. *30–150*

(2 vols., reprint New York: Harper Torchbooks, 1959); A. Momigliano, ed., *The Conflict between Paganism and Christianity in the Fourth Century* (Oxford: Clarendon Press; New York: Oxford University Press, 1963).

XV   The Year One

The only reliable, complete English translation of Josephus appears in Loeb Classical Library (9 vols., 1926–65). I have edited a selection, using that translation, with a long introduction (*Jewish War, and Other Selections from Flavius Josephus*, New York: Washington Square Press, 1965; London: New English Library, 1966). Augustus's own posthumous account of his achievements, the *Res Gestae*, has been newly re-edited with translation and commentary by P. A. Brunt and J. M. Moore (New York and London: Oxford University Press, 1967).

On special topics, see V. Tcherikover, *Hellenistic Civilization and the Jews* (Philadelphia: Jewish Publication Society, 1961); A. H. M. Jones, *The Herods of Judaea* (Oxford: Clarendon Press; New York: Oxford University Press, 1938), *Augustus* (London: Chatto & Windus, 1970; New York: W. W. Norton, 1971); J. Carcopino, *Daily Life in Ancient Rome* (London: Routledge, 1941; Penguin, 1956; New Haven, Conn.: Yale University Press, paperback ed., 1960); L. R. Taylor, *The Divinity of the Roman Emperor* (New York: American Philological Association, 1931); G. E. M. de Ste. Croix, 'Why Were the Early Christians Persecuted?', *Past & Present*, no. 26 (1963), 6–38, with discussion in no. 27 (1964), 23–33; E. A. Thompson, *The Early Germans* (Oxford: Clarendon Press; New York: Oxford University Press, 1965).

INDEX

INDEX

INDEX

INDEX

INDEX

INDEX

INDEX

Thucydides, 26, 44–57, 65, 82, 188

Tiberius, 134, 188, 203, 209

Tiryns, 15

tombs (and tombstones), 96, 102–3, 108, 109, 111, 114–15, 130, 138, 162, 169, 172, 173, 174, 191, 218

trade, 14, 32, 33, 117, 120, 121, 122, 123, 127, 211, 212; *see also under* slaves

tradition, 5, 36–7, 47, 67, 68, 107, 109, 115; Greek, about Crete and Mycenae, 9–10, 35–7; about early Rome, 113, 123, 125–8, 197, 217; *see also* myth

tragedy, 1–6, 25, 47, 90

Trajan, 210–11

treaties, 121, 123, 124, 127

Trojan War, 10, 24–37, 48, 99, 113, 215

Troy, 12, 27, 28, 29–31, 32–5, 36, 113; chronology of, 30–31

Tuscany, 106, 120

Tylissos, 21

Tyndareus, 25

tyranny (and tyrants), 39–41, 47, 75–80, 86, 124, 127–8, 208

Ugarit, 34

Umbria, 106, 120

Uni, 119, 125

Utopia, 77, 151

Valentinian I, 153

Vatican Council, Second, 192–6

Vaughan, Agnes Carr, 102

Ventris, Michael, 18–19

Venus, 27

Vesta, 139, 140

Virgil, 24, 36, 113, 114, 116, 204–5

virtue, *see* morality

Viterbo, 108

Wace, Alan, 17

wages (and fees), 59, 61, 67, 70, 143, 146, 147

war (and peace), 15, 32, 33, 44, 50–1, 82, 99, 113, 116, 117, 121, 122, 124, 139, 145–6, 153, 158, 165, 166–71; civil, 52, 53, 55, 56, 79, 123, 127–8, 145, 156, 194, 202, 205; *see also* arms; mercenaries; Peloponnesian War; Persia and Greece; Trojan War

Wasps (Aristophanes), 61

wealth, 61, 62, 66, 90–2, 94, 95, 116–17, 138, 149, 159, 173, 201

women, 99, 107, 108–9, 129–42, 158, 162, 168, 173, 210; *see also* family; marriage; sexual relations

writing, *see* scripts

Xenophanes, 26

Xenophon, 60–1, 63, 66, 72, 162

Zealots, 194, 201

Zeitlin, Solomon, 193, 194, 195

Zeno, 97

Zeus, 7–10, 25, 27, 47, 118, 119